HEMINGWAY AND FAULKNER

In Their Time

HEMINGWAY
AND
FAULKNER

I N T H E I R T I M E

Edited with Commentary and Narrative by
EARL ROVIT and ARTHUR WALDHORN

continuum
NEW YORK • LONDON

2005

The Continuum International Publishing Group Inc
15 East 26 Street, New York, NY 10010

The Continuum International Publishing Group Ltd
The Tower Building, 11 York Road, London SE1 7NX

Printed in the United States of America

Library of Congress Cataloging-in-Publication Data

Hemingway and Faulkner in their time / edited with commentary and narrative by
Earl Rovit and Arthur Waldhorn.
   p. cm.
  Includes bibliographical references.
  ISBN 0-8264-1687-X (hardcover : alk. paper)
  1. Hemingway, Ernest, 1899–1961—Criticism and interpretation.
2. Faulkner, William, 1897–1962—Criticism and interpretation. 3. Hemingway,
Ernest, 1899–1961—Friends and associates. 4. Faulkner, William,
1897–1962—Friends and associates. I. Waldhorn, Arthur, 1918–
II. Rovit, Earl, 1927–
PS3515.E37Z61775 2005
813'.5209—dc22   2004024767

For Michael Reynolds
and
Paul Smith

"Writers should work alone. They should see each other only after their work is done, and not too often then."

—Ernest Hemingway, *Green Hills of Africa*

"A man works for a fairly simple range of things: money, women, glory; all nice to have but glory's best, and the best of glory is from his peers, like the soldier who has the good opinion not of man but of other soldiers, who are themselves brave too."

—William Faulkner, thanking the American Academy of Art for awarding him the Howells Medal in Fiction, June 1950

CONTENTS

Introduction   13

**1   The 1920s: The Beginnings—Storytellers and
Their Friends in Paris**   21
   Sherwood Anderson (1876–1941); Ernest Hemingway
      (1899–1961); William Faulkner (1897–1962)   23
   Gertrude Stein (1874–1946)   29
   Alice B. Toklas (1877–1967)   32
   F. Scott Fitzgerald (1896–1940)   34
   John Dos Passos (1896–1970)   42
   Archibald MacLeish (1892–1982)   49
   Robert McAlmon (1896–1956)   52
   Isidor Schneider (1896–1977)   54
   Sylvia Beach (1887–1962)   56
   Conrad Aiken (1889–1973)   58
   Harry Crosby (1898–1929)   59
   Edmund Wilson (1895–1972)   62

2   Sounds of the South   73
   John Peale Bishop (1892–1944)   77
   Evelyn Scott (1893–1963)   79
   Caroline Gordon (1895–1981)   80
   Donald Davidson (1893–1968); Allen Tate (1899–1979)   82
   Erskine Caldwell (1903–87)   84
   Cleanth Brooks (1906–94)   86
   John Crowe Ransom (1888–1974)   87
   Thomas Wolfe (1900–38)   87

3   The Poets Sing: On and Off Key   91
   Ezra Pound (1885–1972)   92

T. S. Eliot (1888–1965)   94
William Carlos Williams (1883–1963)   95
Marianne Moore (1887–1972)   96
Louise Bogan (1897–1970)   97
Hart Crane (1899–1932)   98
Carl Sandburg (1878–1967)   99
Wallace Stevens (1879–1955)   100
Robert Frost (1874–1963)   103
Hilda Doolittle [H.D.] (1886–1961)   104
E. E. Cummings (1894–1962)   105
Theodore Roethke (1908–63)   107
Elizabeth Bishop (1911–79)   107

4   Other Voices
The 1930s   109
Theodore Dreiser (1871–1945)   111
H. L. Mencken (1880–1956)   111
Wyndham Lewis (1882–1957)   112
Sinclair Lewis (1885–1951)   114
Katherine Anne Porter (1890–1980)   115
Henry Miller (1891–1980)   118
Dorothy Parker (1893–1967)   118
Josephine Herbst (1897–1969)   120
Glenway Wescott (1901–87)   121
Kay Boyle (1902–92)   122
The 1940s   123
Dashiell Hammett (1894–1961)   124
Thornton Wilder (1897–1975)   125
Dawn Powell (1897–1965)   126
John Steinbeck (1902–68)   128
Hamilton Basso (1904–64)   131
John O'Hara (1905–70)   132
Richard Wright (1908–60)   133
William Saroyan (1908–81)   134
Nelson Algren (1909–81)   135
Wright Morris (1910–98)   136
The 1950s   138
James Thurber (1894–1961)   140
Malcolm Cowley (1898–1989)   141
Kenneth Burke (1897–1993)   141

E. B. White (1899–1985)   143
James T. Farrell (1904–79)   144
Robert Penn Warren (1905–89)   145
W. H. Auden (1907–73)   146
Eudora Welty (1909–2001)   147
Tennessee Williams (1911–83)   148
Mary McCarthy (1912–89)   148
Delmore Schwartz (1913–66)   149
Ralph Ellison (1914–94)   149
Flannery O'Connor (1925–84)   151
Lillian Ross (1927–)   152
Ramon Guthrie (1896–1973)   154

5 **The Exalted Larks**   157
   Hemingway on Faulkner; Faulkner on Hemingway   157

   Bibliographical Materials   169

   Works Cited   177

   Acknowledgments   185

   Photographic Credits   193

   Index   195

Photographs will be found between pages 96 and 97.

INTRODUCTION

THE PERIOD OF 1920 to 1960 was incomparable as a time of glorious flowering in American letters. For probably the last time in our nation's history before images from the small and large screen became the dominant vehicles of social discourse, serious literature entertained a popular readership even as it engaged a truly substantial segment of society in passionate reflection on the issues of the day. It produced seven Nobel Laureates, a distinctly American group of poets who received international recognition, and a resplendent array of fiction writers who inscribed their work on the fabric of those times. Among the latter, Scott Fitzgerald, Thomas Wolfe, John Dos Passos, and John Steinbeck can each justifiably lay claim to eminence—Fitzgerald for the magic of his sentences, Wolfe with his passionate, Niagara-like energy, Dos Passos's authoritative fusion of a keen historical and cinematographic eye, and Steinbeck's measured blend of social insight and compassion. Differing in their unique excellences, they offer a variety of styles and visions that nobly enrich and illuminate their times.

We believe, however, that in terms of enduring influence and intrinsic interest, Hemingway and Faulkner's achievements occupy an even more special tier. And, further, we have come to believe that the work of Hemingway and Faulkner rises like an arch above the work of their variously gifted contemporaries, in part, because of the judgments of those very writers themselves. It is important to remember that the

process through which Hemingway and Faulkner attained that su-
premacy was evaluation by their peers. As Helen Vendler has pointed
out, the establishment of a canon is initially grounded on how writers
feel about and use the work of their strongest predecessors and contemporaries. It is the writers, ultimately, not the critics, scholars, reviewers, or librarians, who originally propel certain bodies of work to
positions of eminence.

Our compilation of the remarks and responses of Hemingway's
and Faulkner's contemporaries—a slightly dissonant chorus of voices
which, somewhat grandiloquently, we think of as an exaltation of
larks—though far from exhaustive, is significant. It demonstrates, for
one thing, the importance of their role in recognizing and promoting
the worth of these two "promising" young writers, or, to recast the
title of George Meredith's poem, larks ascending. The letters and
journal entries reveal—and this is a second facet of their importance—
both an intuitive and considered understanding of the strengths as
well as the fault lines on which Hemingway and Faulkner were building their houses of fiction. No matter that Faulkner's work was
largely out-of-print by the time Malcolm Cowley edited *The Portable
Faulkner* in 1946 or that Hemingway's popularity by the end of the
1930s had more perhaps to do with his lifestyle than his work. Their
fellow writers were keenly aware of the roots of each man's genius,
the moral concerns that underlay the artistry of their expression.

In the past half-century, biographers have scrutinized their daily
lives for clues that might define their genius. Hemingway, the gregarious, "regular guy" public figure; Faulkner, almost reclusive, patri-
cian, protectively private—what do they share? On a simple level,
each believed himself to be capable of becoming a great—even an
"immortal" writer, if only he could devote his energies single-mind-
edly enough to that end. Both were intensely competitive and remained so throughout their lives. Both—with greater or lesser

justification—complained constantly about a lack of money (Faulkner writing to a friend that he is "about run out of mules to mortgage"). Surely not enough to discriminate them from one another or, for that matter, from many of their peers. But even when one probes deeper, questions remain unanswered. "SuperPapa," as John Updike called Hemingway, still remains hidden beneath the layers of his irresolute gender, his self-confident male independence a pose belied by his fiction where all things end badly and no man can go it alone. Nevertheless, in tight-lipped postures of resolution which became iconic for a generation, Hemingway's characters never forsake the journey. Nor do Faulkner's. Despite his lifelong alcoholic depressions coupled with a clear-sighted glimpse into the nihilistic abyss he knew to be an integral part of the human enterprise, his disciplined belief in life never abated. His refusal, in his acceptance of the Nobel Prize, "to accept the end of man" and his declaration that "man will not merely endure: he will prevail" attest to the humanistic faith that was the foundation of the labyrinth of dubieties which layer his work and, paradoxically, add to the power of its ultimate affirmation.

It would be a mistake, however, to over-emphasize the distinction between Hemingway's seeming gregariousness and Faulkner's relative reclusiveness. Although it is true that Hemingway appears to have always been the lively center of one or another partying group—hunting and fishing in Upper Michigan, making the rounds of the bistros and sports arenas in Paris, the bullrings of Spain, the safaris in Africa, or trolling the Gulf Stream—Faulkner certainly never lacked friends who were eager to embrace his company. After his first foray into the bohemian life of New Orleans, he found easy acceptance both in the Greenwich Village milieu and among the extended Algonquin group and its westward spillover among the writers who had journeyed to the Eldorado of the Hollywood studios. Each man had a plethora of drinking and hunting companions. The main difference seems to have been that Hemingway's friends regarded themselves more often than not as boon companions—intimates—and were in various degrees surprised and hurt to find themselves shelved or, in some cases, attacked as enemies. This somehow didn't happen with Faulkner. His much-remarked "courtesy" and reserved demeanor afforded him a social distance, even as it protected his privacy and preserved a feeling of respect in relation to his associates. And while he was certainly not loved so intensely as was Hemingway, he engendered nothing of the rancor which stained so many of Hemingway's relationships.

In this context, it is permissible, we believe, to speculate briefly on the degree to which the figures who people their fiction may provide a key to the hidden authors behind the artistic veil. Obviously every character a writer produces—even those overly dependent on stereotypes—is, in some aspect, a deliberate or inadvertent projection of a personality whom the writer thinks or wishes or dreads he might be. To imagine another human being, after all—to construct his or her DNA in cogent language—is not only to form, but to perform that personality; to assume the nature of an Other drawn from one's own psychic marrow.

Even as we are aware of the danger of falling into the quicksand of the biographical fallacy, we inevitably assume that some of these vivid simulacra hew closer to the bone than others. How much of Hemingway is really incarnate in Nick Adams? in Francis Macomber? in Pilar? in Santiago? To what degree is Faulkner Quentin Compson? Gowan or Gavin Stevens? Addie Bundren? Joe Christmas? Without getting into an inconclusive—albeit, fascinating—parlor game, these speculations suggest one possibly surprising truth.

The most persuasively vital characters of both authors seem to us unusually lonely people. Whether as first-person narrators who speak for themselves or characters seen from the outside as active agents, they tend to exist on the peripheries of the action. We watch them observing others or observing themselves being acted-upon in a kind of removed double vision. And perhaps this is not so surprising after all. The writing of fiction is a singularly solitary pursuit, and one that has to be sustained over weeks and months of willed solitude. We ought to expect, therefore, a significant transference from the isolated consciousness that frames and puts into motion and emotion the mis-en-scène and the projected human simulations which enact it.

Doubtless this is a condition common to all serious artists, nor can one know whether this voluntary alienation is the cause of the creative impulse or the reverse. But it seems to us that despite the vast differences in their lives and personalities, in their labor to attain the exalted Everest of their aspirations, both Hemingway and Faulkner had to struggle all their lives to negotiate a passage through a proportionately treacherous Khumbu Icefall of hollow isolation. Their resort to excessive alcohol, their intractable difficulties in establishing intimacy with other human beings, Hemingway's need to seek a kind of oblivion in situations of extreme physical risk, and Faulkner's draconian preservation of a sort of armored privacy—these desperate survival tactics locked them into what appears to be a remarkably shared identity. There is, we think, a fateful sameness that haunts their characters' experience even as it so cruelly bedeviled the lives of their creators.

New critical and biographical materials will undoubtedly appear, each offering fresh theories of personality and creativity. What will remain is the extraordinary body of *work* they produced and that is the focus of our book. Their peers gossiped incessantly about Hemingway and Faulkner, and our "larks" made less than pleasant comments not only about some of their peers but about one another as well. What makes this compilation significant, however, is not the biographical detail, necessary and often fascinating as it is, but what their peers and they themselves recognized about the significance of their writing. That they were creating styles radically different from any that had preceded them; that they were peopling their stories and novels with characters who might help readers understand what they and life were like between 1920 and 1960. They were both *modern* writers who, though skeptical and ironic, rejected what we today call *postmodern,* the senselessly impersonal denial of historical and ethical values. Hemingway with his simplicity, Faulkner with his swirling rhetoric ripped away the fancy décor that hid whatever they thought false, unethical, or destructive in American life. Their peers often heard what the "larks" were singing about before the rest of America heard.

Finally, there resides in this compilation an intrinsic pleasure in the spontaneous reactions of all these extraordinary people as well as in their often lengthy and carefully reasoned responses. They are passionate, engaged, supportive, envious, articulate, self-revealing—and wonderfully human. Criticism and scholarship as we too often encounter them, have metastasized into bewildering clusters and fragments of methodology and theory. But what yet remains of fruitful discussion about Hemingway and Faulkner in the early twenty-first century has grown from seeds planted in the 1920s by their fellow tillers—agrarian and urban. The vintage of that literary soil we have affectionately gathered in this book.

The organizing structure of our work should become clear as the reader pursues its sentences. The prefatory observations that follow may, however, facilitate the process.

We have assembled—from letters, journals, diaries, interviews, and other forms of commentary—a representative gathering of the private and semi-public remarks made by their contemporaries and immediate successors, including the "charmed circle" in Paris, the New Yorkers, the Chicagoans, the Hollywood bunch, and—from Nashville, New Orleans, Richmond, and elsewhere—those who took their stand in Southernism.

The cross-influences among these writers are incredibly complex, often reciprocal, and rich in stylistic, thematic, and historical implication. We have often prefaced sections with interludes, brief accounts of how our writers met one another—more common with the gregarious Hemingway than with the polite but insulated Faulkner. Since most of them certainly knew the achievements of their contemporaries, any attempt to chart their collective aesthetic assessment is easily muddled by their rivalry and friendships. We have tried to restrict our focus to the writers' literary responses to Hemingway and Faulkner, but have on occasion succumbed to temptation and included spiteful gossip and fulsome flattery, also allowing the writers (including Hemingway and Faulkner) to state their zestful personal resentments and prejudices. Whenever relationships or situations become hopelessly entangled, we provide an explanatory interlude within, rather than prefatory, to the text.

In the final section, using narrative as well as direct quotation, we let Hemingway and Faulkner respond to one another and try to voice their own sense of the complex relationship that bound them comfortlessly for four decades.

Hemingway's bluster and blatant competitiveness drew far more response from his peers than did Faulkner's reticence. In fact, most of our writers tend to have registered Faulkner's achievements with the quiet appreciation of spectators watching a performance at a distance. Unlike Hemingway, Faulkner was remote from their personal lives, even as his style and content occupied, as it were, a venue they had no intention of entering. Also, unlike Hemingway, Faulkner did not often vent his evaluations of his competitors' accomplishments. Consequently, the relative dominance of references to Hemingway in our

survey in no way diminishes the complexity of the drama that enmeshed the two men.

Among the novelists and poets whose voices report from these
scattered precincts, a few speak but once. Edith Wharton, for example, the grande dame of American letters nearing the end of her career,
wrote to a friend in 1934: "What a country! With Faulkner and Hemingway acclaimed as the greatest American novelists, & magazine editors still taking the view they did when I began to write! Brains &
culture seem nonexistent from one end of the social scale to the
other, & half the morons yell for filth, & the other half continue to
put pants on piano-legs." In yet another example of a single response,
Sara Teasdale, the shy St. Louis poet, wrote to her husband: "I was
amused by your account of the people in 'The Sun Also Rises.' I'm
afraid I couldn't stand them even in a book." (William Drake, *Sara
Teasdale: A Woman and a Poet*, 247).

Most writers, however, comment more often, some pronouncing
their views throughout the four decades represented in the text. Entries within each section follow a more or less chronological order.

ONE

The 1920s:
The Beginnings—Storytellers and
Their Friends in Paris

*P*erhaps the simplest way to describe one of the cultural consequences of America's intervention in World War I is that it set thousands of young men and women into motion. The immediate brief postwar economic boom, the proliferation of radio, and the rapid conquest of the American heartland by the automobile effectively destroyed traditional nineteenth century rural-and-village life, draining the hinterlands and swelling the industrial centers and, as a byproduct, establishing small bohemian enclaves across the country. Hardly a good-sized town lacked such a venue, often centered around a bookshop and a local college. Such communities—however fragile—announced their existence with a little magazine—itself equally ephemeral. Wherever they were, however, their models were elsewhere—to some extent, San Francisco or Chicago, but, more usually, the French Quarter of New Orleans and, preeminently, with its proximity to the publishing industry, Greenwich Village. The most alluring Bohemia, of course, was Paris, dream-cheap in relation to the American dollar, immune to Comstockery and Prohibition, and storied in its romantic appeal.

". . . Paris, France, that is where we all were, and it was natural for us to be there," wrote Gertrude Stein, who had established her salon before the war. "For the first time since the 18th century, civilization was more important than sentiment, fashion more important than realism. And so we all lived in France because the French have always been civilized, logical and fashionable. And so we had to be there and we were all there." (*We Moderns: 1920–1940*, 3). With a more critically oriented point of view, Stein might have been describing what historians define as modernism. Given the exciting contributions of its artists and philosophers, Paris was certainly the nexus of the assaults on traditional approaches to literature and culture that are basic components of modernism. Moreover, as Leslie Fiedler has written, "they had the nerve proper to their excesses. . . ." ("The Ant and the Grasshopper," *Partisan Review*, 415).

Americans of what was later to be theatrically dubbed "The Lost Generation" varied in their attitudes to the War and expatriation. Some who had served in France returned happily to the States, settling into thoroughly successful careers (Louis Bromfield, E. E. Cummings, John Crowe Ransom, Harold Ross, Harry Truman, DeWitt Wallace, Edmund Wilson). Others who had enlisted but had never been sent overseas (like Scott Fitzgerald, but unlike Henry Luce) always regretted missing out on the war. And many, of course, seized the opportunity to make a run on the Left Bank as an escape from the strictures of home and community (Kay Boyle, Henry Miller, Malcolm Cowley, Hart Crane, Robert McAlmon). What they all had in common—more than anything else—was a sense of membership in an age-group-related experience that transcended regional and religious backgrounds.

Ernest Hemingway, who had been severely wounded on the Italian front, worked as a reporter for the *Toronto Star*, and, newly married, arrived in Paris in 1922, prepared to launch himself as a major writer of fiction. By 1923, he had published six poems in *Poetry* and later that year his first book, *Three Stories and Ten Poems*. His first novel, *The Sun Also Rises*, appeared in 1926. William Faulkner, who had joined the Royal Air Force in Canada but had never been sent overseas, spent some months in Paris in 1925, but scrupulously avoided the Left Bank scene, preferring to walk the boulevards and visit the museums alone. As he wrote his mother (September 22, 1925), "I have spent afternoon after afternoon in the Louvre—and in the Luxembourg; I have seen Rodin's museum and 2 private collections of Matisse and Picasso (who are yet alive and painting) as well as numberless young and struggling moderns. And Cézanne! That man dipped his brush in light like Tobe Caruthers would dip his in red lead to paint a lamp-post. . . ." (Blotner, *Selected Letters*, 24).

In 1924, he published *The Marble Faun*, a volume of poems, his first novel, *Soldier's Pay*, in 1926, and, a year later, a more substantial effort, *Mosquitoes*. In their late twenties, with several legitimate publications in print, the fledgling larks had begun their flights.

Sherwood Anderson (1876–1941), Ernest Hemingway (1899–1961), and William Faulkner (1897–1962)

Personal relations between Anderson and Hemingway were short lived but of enormous value to the younger man. They met in Chicago in January, 1921, two years after Anderson's *Winesburg, Ohio* had established him at the age of forty-three as a major American writer. Hemingway was twenty-two, writing and editing copy for a trade journal, courting Hadley Richardson, and floundering for direction as a writer. The two men met through happenstance: Hemingway's roommate, Kenley (elder brother of Hemingway's boyhood friend, Bill Smith), and Anderson worked for the same advertising firm. Kenley suggested a meeting, Anderson agreed and, for the next four months, during encounters at Anderson's apartment in Chicago and home in suburban Palos Park, Hemingway absorbed Anderson's discourse about modern art, American writing (with particular emphasis upon Mark Twain and Walt Whitman), contemporary literary gossip, and critiques of his own work. About to leave with his wife for Paris, Anderson encouraged a like path for Hemingway and assured him meetings with Gertrude Stein and Ezra Pound, each already established in the expatriate world of the Left Bank. Thereafter, Hemingway and Anderson—for reasons the correspondence below may suggest—never met, except casually.

As with Hemingway, Faulkner's meeting with Anderson was the product of fortuities. In 1921, friends from Oxford, Mississippi (Phil Stone and Stark Young) had helped Faulkner get a job in New York as a salesman for the Doubleday shop in Lord & Taylor's department store. The manager of the store, Elizabeth Prall, would later become Sherwood Anderson's second wife. Prall liked the young man but also noted that he drank too much. Thus, by the time Faulkner arrived in New Orleans three years later, Anderson—recently married to Prall and himself a new resident in the city—knew who Faulkner was and, as he had with Hemingway, served as a gracious and significant mentor, personally recommending the publication of Faulkner's first novel, *Soldier's Pay,* with his own publisher, Boni and Liveright. Like Hemingway, Faulkner originally sought Paris and would spend time there in 1925, but without availing himself of the opportunities to meet Gertrude Stein or mingle with the group soon to become her Lost Generation.

Anderson on Hemingway:

> Mr. Hemingway is young, strong, full of laughter, and he can write. Blurb for *In Our Time* (1925).

Anderson had written to Liveright in June about "young Bill Faulkner as the one writer of promise" in New Orleans. When Liveright accepted Faulkner's *Soldier's Pay*, he wrote again (August 28, 1925):

> I'm glad you're going to publish Faulkner's novel. I have a hunch he's a comer. . . . (*The Letters of Sherwood Anderson*, eds. Howard Mumford Jones and Walter Rideout, 146).

The publisher, Horace Liveright (1886–1933), is described satirically—but accurately—by Waldo Frank in *The New Yorker*: "He has sponsored half the advanced novelists who pollute our homes, half the radical thinkers who defile our customs, half the free verse poets who corrupt our English." (Cited in Tom Dardis: *Firebrand: The Life of Horace Liveright*, 121). Besides Anderson, Hemingway, and Faulkner, Liveright's authors included Djuna Barnes, Hart Crane, Cummings, Dreiser, T. S. Eliot, Freud, Robinson Jeffers, Joyce, O'Neill, and Ezra Pound. The Modern Library was also his creation, a series he later sold to one of his former employees.

In partnership with Albert and Charles Boni, the flamboyant Liveright—an inveterate and successful womanizer, gambler, and rotten businessman—became the third Jewish publisher (after Ben Huebsch and Alfred A. Knopf) to breach the solidly conservative Protestant publishing industry. Like his co-religionists who built Hollywood or promoted jazz during the 1920s, Liveright had an acute sense of what seemed "new" and willingly took huge risks on his judgments. His failures as a Broadway producer and as an investor during the Crash of 1929 drove him from publishing in 1930. Three years later, unable to recoup his fortunes in Hollywood, he died of pneumonia. Ezra Pound, an unlikely source of praise for either Jews or businessmen, nevertheless described Liveright as "a pearl among publishers."

Faulkner on his and Hemingway's satirical parodies of Anderson (*Mosquitoes*, *Sherwood Anderson & Other Creoles*, and *The Torrents of Spring*):

> Neither of us "could have touched, ridiculed, his work itself . . . but we had made his style look ridiculous; and by that time . . . he too must have known in his heart that there was nothing else left." (Joseph Blotner, *Faulkner: A Biography*, 536).

Faulkner on Anderson: From the Dedication to *Sartoris* (1929):

> To Sherwood Anderson, through whose kindness I was first published.

Anderson on Hemingway (Letter to Ralph Church, 13 January 1936):

> I began reading Hemmy's Green Hills of Africa and thinking of him . . . It's really a lousy book, and the god awful thing is that he doesn't know it and never will. . . . There's the whole world of men he can't get at all; so he proclaims his superiority to it and them. And then too, he's too concerned with writing. Thinks of it too much like the eternal amateur he is and always will be, the small bad boy. 'Kiss my ass' he cries in ecstasy and then is heartbroken because we don't see any sense to it and won't. I think it's rather like this . . . Of course every man has a hell of a time. First he has to work to get someone else, usually some woman, out from between him and his canvas. That's a fight. Then he has to try to get himself out. That's the thing

Hemmy can't do. (*Letters of Sherwood Anderson*, eds. Howard Mumford Jones and Walter Rideout, 345).

Diary entry (27 October 1937):

. . . went to Max Perkins. We sat in a café and he told me the story of the fight between Hemingway and Eastman . . . a very silly affair. From Max's story it was pretty much Hemingway's childishness. (*The Sherwood Anderson Diaries*, ed. Hilbert H. Campbell, 135).

In June, 1933, Max Eastman (1883–1969), a co-founder of the radical magazine, *New Masses*, had written an unenthusiastic review of Hemingway's *Death in the Afternoon*, pungently titled "Bull in the Afternoon." Among other humorously intended remarks, he accused Hemingway of overly protesting his "red-blooded masculinity" and assuming "a literary style . . . of wearing false hair on the chest." The review festered in Hemingway's mind for over four years, finally bursting in August, 1937, when Hemingway and Eastman met by accident in Max Perkins's office at Scribner's: Hemingway unbuttoned his shirt to show his chest and then slapped Eastman in the face with a book. The fracas ended as both men fell across Perkins's desk to the floor, Eastman atop a now smiling Hemingway.

Anderson on Faulkner: In a letter to Laura Copenhaver (11 November 1937) Anderson wrote that he had been called to the Algonquin Hotel where Faulkner had been found wandering through the corridors naked after a week-long drunk. A few days earlier, thinking about Hemingway and Faulkner, Anderson had written:

There is this sharp difference between the man [Hemingway] and, say Wolfe or Faulkner. They may write of terrible happenings, but you feel always an inner sympathy with the fact of life itself. (*Letters*, 393).

Anderson on Faulkner:

I knew Bill Faulkner before his name had become known in the world of scribblers. I was living down in the old French Quarter in New Orleans when Bill came there from . . . Oxford, Mississippi . . . I used to hear his typewriter rattling away . . . He was always pounding at it, pounding away . . .

He was the story teller but he was something else too. The man is what they mean in the South when they use the word "gentle" . . . Life may be at times infinitely vulgar. Bill never is. He is the story teller doing his story teller's job. As I read Bill often the conviction comes that it is in the moonlight and magnolia blossom writing that the real vulgarity lies. (*We Moderns: 1920–1940*, 29).

Although the quality of Anderson's work perceptibly declined through the 1930s, younger writers—including Thomas Wolfe, Hamilton Basso, and Paul Green—continued to seek him out. "It seems," he wrote, after a visit to John Steinbeck's ranch in 1939, "I've become a kind of Papa, 'Reading you is what started me writing,' etc. etc., so I sit like a wise owl." (Cited in Townsend, 309). Paralleling this experience, in a sense, is the young Shelby Foote telling Faulkner in 1951: "When you began, you had Sherwood Anderson and Conrad to learn from. But I'm luckier. I've got you and Proust." (Blotner, 1414).

At the end of February, 1941, Anderson set out on a semi-official goodwill trip to Latin America. Shortly before the sailing, he appar-

THE 1920s: THE BEGINNINGS

ently swallowed a toothpick which penetrated his intestine and caused peritonitis. By the time his ship reached the Canal Zone on March 4, he was in severe pain (Thornton Wilder was aboard and tried futilely to help) and died a few days later.

Faulkner on Anderson (in *The Atlantic Monthly*, 1953):

> He was warm, generous, merry and fond of laughing, without pettiness and jealous only of the integrity which he believed to be absolutely necessary in anyone who approached his craft. . . . (cited in Townsend, 220).

Hemingway on Anderson (Letter to Harvey Breit, July 3, 1956):

> Sherwood was like a jolly but tortured bowl of puss [*sic*] turning into a woman in front of your eyes . . . (*Ernest Hemingway, Selected Letters*, ed. Carlos Baker, 862).

Faulkner on Anderson (Interview at Washington and Lee University, May 15, 1958):

> In my opinion, he's the father of all of my generation— Hemingway, Erskine Caldwell, Thomas Wolfe, Dos Passos. Of course Mark Twain is the grandfather. But Sherwood Anderson–in my opinion has still to receive his rightful place in American letters." (*Faulkner in the University*, eds. Frederick Gwynn and Joseph Blotner, 281).

Gertrude Stein (1874–1946)

Two months after the newly wed Hemingway arrived in Paris in Spring of 1922, he sent Gertrude Stein the letter of introduction Sherwood

Anderson had written for him. Stein's reply was prompt and gracious, a warm invitation for the couple to have tea with her and Alice B. Toklas at their apartment on 27 rue de Fleurus, a residence and salon famed for its collection of modern art and literary celebrities.

Faulkner was in Paris in 1925 but never visited Stein or any of the other literary lions of the day. He preferred to walk the city alone. Stein makes no reference to him either in her writings or her correspondence. (But see Alice Toklas below.) Faulkner's attitude toward the expatriate scene may be partly explained by his sardonic and prescient comments in a 1922 review:

> Writing people are . . . pathetically torn between a desire to make a figure in the world and a morbid interest in their personal egos. . . . And with characteristic national restlessness, those with imagination and some talent find it unbearable. O'Neill has turned his back on America to write of the sea. Marsden Hartley explodes vindictive firecrackers in Montmartre. Alfred Kreymborg has gone to Italy, and Ezra Pound furiously toys with spurious bronze in London. All have found America aesthetically impossible; yet, being of America, will some day return, a few into dyspeptic exile, others to write joyously for the movies. ("Books & Things," *The Mississippian*, 5, Feb. 3, 1922. Reprinted in *William Faulkner: Early Prose and Poetry*, ed. Carvel Collins, 94).

> I remember very well the impression I had of Hemingway that first afternoon. [March, 1922] He was an extraordinarily good-looking young man . . . rather foreign looking, with passionately interested, rather than interesting eyes. (*The Autobiography of Alice B. Toklas*. Page references are to the text as published in *Selected Writings of Gertrude Stein*, ed. Carl Van Vechten, 176).

Stein's comment to Hemingway after reading "Up in Michigan":

> 'It's good,' she said, 'That's not the question at all. But it is *inaccrochable*. That means it's like a picture that a painter paints and

then he cannot hang it when he has a show and nobody will buy because they cannot hang it either. . . . You mustn't write anything that is *inaccrochable*. There is no point in it. It's wrong and it's silly.' (Ernest Hemingway, *A Moveable Feast*, 15).

She always says, yes sure I have a weakness for Hemingway. After all he was the first of the young men to knock at my door and he did make [Ford Madox] Ford print the first piece of The Making of Americans. (*Toklas*, 178).

Hemingway corrected the proofs, a task from which he "learned a great deal and he admired all that he learned." (*Toklas*, 179). Hemingway's response: Some passages had "great brilliance," but she wrote "endlessly in repetitions that a more conscientious and less lazy writer would have put in the waste basket." (*A Moveable Feast*, 17–18).

Gertrude Stein and Sherwood Anderson are very funny on the subject of Hemingway . . . Hemingway had been formed by the two of them and they were both a little proud and a little ashamed of the work of their minds . . . it is so flattering to have a pupil who does it without understanding it, in other words he takes training and anybody who takes training is a favorite pupil. . . . And that is Hemingway, he looks like a modern and he smells of the museums. (*Toklas*, 179).

They (Anderson and Stein) admitted that Hemingway was

yellow . . . just like the flat boat men on the Mississippi River as described by Mark Twain. But what a book, they both agreed, would be the real story of Hemingway, not those he writes but the confessions of the real Ernest Hemingway . . . but alas he never will. After all, as he himself once murmured, there is the career, the career. (*Toklas*, 179).

Stein's comment, "You are all a lost generation" is enmeshed in controversy, stemming from a passing remark she made to Hemingway on her garage owner's observation about ill-trained young mechanics. The most coherent account is in James R. Mellow's *Charmed Circle: Gertrude Stein and Company*, 273–75. Hemingway considered *The Lost Generation* as the title for *The Sun Also Rises*. The actual "Foreword" to a version entitled *The Lost Generation* is quoted in Reynolds, *Hemingway: The Paris Years*, 327.

The coda to the complex love-hate relationship between Stein and Hemingway begins in Hemingway's *Paris Review* "Interview" [May, 1954]:

> Miss Stein wrote at some length and with considerable inaccuracy about her influence on my work. It was necessary for her to do this after she had learned to write dialogue from a book called *The Sun Also Rises*. I was very fond of her and thought it was splendid she had learned to write conversation. It was no new thing for me to learn from everyone I could, living or dead, and I had no idea it would affect Gertrude so violently. (George Plimpton, ed. *Writers at Work: Second Series*, 227).

The second part of the one-two punch sequence is the gratuitously cruel chapter, "A Strange Enough Ending," (*A Moveable Feast*) wherein Hemingway delivers the last word.

Alice B. Toklas (1877–1967)

In 1903, Gertrude Stein returned with her brother to the Paris where she had spent much of her childhood. Four years later, Alice B. Toklas arrived from California with a friend who knew the Steins and had whetted Toklas's interest in their art collection. Toklas was thirty-one, Stein thirty-three when they met. The attraction was mutual, immediate, and permanent.

Letter to Carl Van Vechten (December 19, 1946):

> . . . I think that the generation is finished—it really ended with Fitzgerald . . . However good Faulkner may be he isn't virile— and as for poor Hem and Steinbeck and the rest of them—the less said the better for one's digestion. (*Letters of Alice B. Toklas: Staying on Alone*, ed. Edward Burns, 38).

Letter to Fernanda Pivano (July 4, 1950):

> Gertrude liked *Sanctuary* but didn't like the next two and wouldn't try any more. She didn't see any influence of her work in *Sanctuary*. But I see a considerable influence (conscious or unconscious?) in *Intruder*. (*Letters*, 194).

Letter to Fernanda Pivano (Oct. 10, 1950):

> . . . The present Hemingway crack up—one must borrow from the vocabulary of the greatest of his victims—has far too much old biblical punishments and rewards for comfort to those living in the present. But of course that is just what he doesn't do—he is hopelessly 1890—and one can damn him no further. He wears like the new look but he is in the tradition of Kipling. . . . (*Letters*, 210).

Letter to Samuel Steward (August 7, 1958):

> You know Gertrude told Hemingway—in the early days—he couldn't earn his living doing newspaper work and write—he

should like Sherwood [Anderson] earn his living running a laundry. (*Letters*, 364. See also entry below under Lillian Ross).

F. Scott Fitzgerald (1896–1940)

Fitzgerald and Hemingway met in Paris in the Spring of 1925, just a few months after Fitzgerald—fresh from the triumph of *The Great Gatsby*—called Maxwell Perkins's (his editor at Scribner's) attention to Hemingway's talent. Each admired the other but neither, as Michael Reynolds has noted, realized that one of them had already "passed his zenith on a curve heading down into professional and personal darkness." Nor was Hemingway aware "of the approaching magnitude of his career whose curve was only beginning to move toward its peak." (Reynolds, *The Paris Years*, 282). Affection as well as personal and artistic jealousy colored their relationship, Hemingway's behavior the less forgivable as Fitzgerald's decline became more precipitous.

Faulkner's noted indifference to the world of the Parisian café and salon during the 1920s precluded his meeting Fitzgerald. Both men worked intermittently in Hollywood during the 1930s but despite the fact that both were there between 1937 and 1940 (when Fitzgerald died), no indication exists that they ever met. Neither was ever more than a journeyman screenwriter, though Fitzgerald from the outset worked on more substantial assignments, sometimes writing treatments and at least beginning an occasional script. Most important was that Fitzgerald's experience in Hollywood provided him—as it did not for Faulkner—with material for a novel he never lived to complete, one which nevertheless proved that despite his "crackup," Fitzgerald's creative genius yet breathed. In *The Last Tycoon*, Fitzgerald's central character, Monroe Stahr, lives as a dramatic portrait far beyond his real-life "model," the brilliant young Hollywood producer, Irving Thalberg.

Between 1932 and 1945, Faulkner's chief sources of income were sporadic screenwriting contracts with MGM, 20th Century Fox, Warner Brothers, and others—partly secured by the respect and affection with which Howard Hawks regarded him. It was hackwork that Faulkner performed professionally with neither pride nor satisfaction except for the much-needed paychecks. "I'm a motion-picture doctor," he once described himself. "I reworked sections. I don't write scripts." (Tom Dardis, *Some Time in the Sun*, 108). One probably apocryphal tale relates that at a story-conference, the problem was how to establish at the beginning of the film the impossibility of a consummated romance between the young hero and heroine who are in love with one another. Faulkner, puffing his omnipresent pipe, remarked laconically, "Make them brother and sister." In an interview with Joel Sayre, one of Faulkner's screenwriting collaborators, Sayre recalled Mencken's telling him that "this boy [Faulkner] is a wonderful comedy writer." (Blotner, 924). It is curious to note that Mencken's appreciative comment on Faulkner's comic talent—surely a significant part of his work—is one of the rare recorded recognitions of this aspect of his genius.

Introduced by Nathanael West to the shifting group of sometime-screenwriters who met casually at Stanley Rose's bookshop on Hollywood Boulevard (among them Dashiell Hammett, John O'Hara, Erskine Caldwell, Gene Fowler, Horace McCoy, and Stephen Longstreet), Faulkner remained characteristically courteous and aloof, becoming friendly with West and Hawks who shared his passion for wild-game hunting. West was bemused that Faulkner always called him "Mr. West" and Faulkner was gratified that West liked *Sanctuary.* Faulkner also established a sustained liaison with Meta Carpenter, a script clerk who worked for Hawks. (The fullest treatment of Faulkner's Hollywood experience is Tom Dardis, *Some Time in the Sun*, 80–149. See also Meta Carpenter Wilde and Orin Borsten, *A Loving Gentleman: The Love Story of William Faulkner and Meta Carpenter*).

In 1943, Faulkner began but apparently never succeeded in completing a film script based on Fitzgerald's short story, "The Curious Case of Benjamin Button." Faulkner was still writing scripts in the early 1950s.

Letter to Max Perkins (before Oct. 18,1924):

> This is to tell you about a young man named Ernest Hemingway, who lives in Paris (an American), writes for the *Transatlantic Review* and has a brilliant future. Ezra Pound published a collection of his short pieces in Paris . . . He's the real thing. (Andrew Turnbull, ed. *The Letters of F. Scott Fitzgerald*, 167).

Letter to Max Perkins on *The Torrents of Spring* (Dec. 30, 1925):

> I loved it, but believe it wouldn't be popular . . . the book is almost a vicious parody on him. You see I agree with Ernest that Anderson's last two books have let everybody down who believed in him—I think they're cheap, faked, obscurantic, and awful. (Turnbull, 195).

Max Perkins (Maxwell Evarts Perkins, 1884–1947) spent almost forty years at Charles Scribner's, most of it earning his reputation as America's most respected editor. "Don't ever *defer* to my judgment," he wrote to Fitzgerald, ". . . a writer must speak solely for himself." He threatened to resign if Charles Scribner denied Hemingway the right to use "bitch" to describe Brett Ashley in *The Sun Also Rises*. He tolerated Thomas Wolfe's explosiveness and random narrative trajectories, gently bringing him more or less back on track, always patient with the writer he loved most as a talented if wayward child. He fostered talents as diverse as Marjorie Kinnan Rawlings (*The Yearling*, 1938) and James Jones, his last "discovery," whose rough draft for the novel that would become *From Here to Eternity* (1951) Perkins rejected in 1945—but included a substantial advance encouraging him to complete the novel.

Perkins's authors quibbled among themselves and complained bitterly about their royalties, but their loyalty to their editor, though occasionally strained, inevitably triumphed because each of them believed in what Perkins wrote to Hemingway, words that shaped the title of the Hemingway-Perkins correspondence: ". . . the utterly real thing in writing is the only thing that counts." (See Matthew J. Bruccoli, *The Only Thing That Counts*, 1996).

After a Riviera conversation in which Fitzgerald urged . . . Glenway Westcott to help promote Hemingway's reputation, Westcott concluded that Fitzgerald's admiration for Hemingway damaged Fitzgerald by convincing him he could delegate literary responsibilities to Hemingway. (Matthew J. Bruccoli, *Some Sort of Epic Grandeur: The Life of F. Scott Fitzgerald*, 248–49).

Letter to Max Perkins (June 25, 1926) about *The Sun Also Rises*:

I liked it but with certain qualifications. The fiesta, the fishing trip, the minor characters were fine. The lady I didn't like, perhaps because I don't like the original. In the mutilated man I thought Ernest bit off more than can yet be chewn between the covers of a book, then lost his nerve a little and edited the more vitalizing details out. . . . (Turnbull, 205–6).

For an account of Fitzgerald's pre-publication ten-page critique of the novel, see, among others, Bruccoli, *Epic Grandeur*, 249–250, and Frederic Joseph Svoboda, *Hemingway & The Sun Also Rises: The Crafting of a Style*, 98, 100–105. For Fitzgerald's nine-page memo of editorial suggestions for *A Farewell to Arms*, some of which Hemingway used, but never acknowledged, see Bruccoli, *Epic Grandeur*, 274–78.

In a journal note (1930), Fitzgerald confesses that:

> he'd begun to think of himself during 1925 and 1926 . . . as a man of the world and had decided 'that everybody liked me and admired me for myself but I only liked a few people like Ernest and Charlie McArthur and Gerald and Sara [Murphy] who were my peers. . . . I woke up in Hollywood no longer my egotistic certain self but a mixture of Ernest in fine clothes and Gerald with a career—and Charlie McArthur with a past. (Cited in Scott Donaldson, *Fool for Love*, 55).

Letter to Max Perkins (May, 1932):

> . . . if the last five years uncovered Ernest, Tom and Faulkner it would have been worthwhile. . . . (Turnbull, 227).

Letter to Max Perkins (Jan. 19, 1933):

> I was in New York for three days last week on a terrible bat. . . . Am going on the water-wagon from the first of February to the first of April but don't tell Ernest because he has long convinced himself that I am an incurable alcoholic. . . . I am *his* alcoholic just like Ring [Lardner] is mine and do not want to disillusion him. . . . (Turnbull, 230).

Letter to Max Perkins (March 4, 1934):

> After all, Max, I am a plodder. One time I had a talk with EH, and I told him that I was the tortoise and he was the hare, and that's the truth of the matter, that everything I have ever attained has been through long and persistent struggle while it is Ernest who has a touch of genius which enables him to bring off extraordinary things with facility. I have no facility. I have a facility for being cheap, if I wanted to indulge that. (Turnbull, 247).

Letter to John Peale Bishop (April 7, 1934):

> I believe it was EH who developed to me, in conversation, that the dying fall was preferable to the dramatic ending under certain conditions, and I think we both got the germ of the idea from Conrad. (Turnbull, 363).

Letter to Hemingway (June 1, 1934):

> I think it is obvious that my respect for your artistic life is absolutely unqualified, that save for a few of the dead or dying old men you are the only man writing fiction in America that I look up to very much. (Cited in Bruccoli, *Epic Grandeur*, 377).

Letter to Max Perkins on similarities linking Hemingway with himself and Thomas Wolfe (July 30, 1934):

> What family resemblance there is between we three as writers is the attempt that crops up in our fiction from time to time to recapture the exact feel of a moment in time and space, exemplified by people rather than by things—that is, an attempt at what Wordsworth was trying to do rather than what Keats did with

such magnificent ease, an attempt at a mature memory of a deep experience. (Turnbull, 251).

Letter to Max Perkins (September 19, 1936) concerning the magazine publication of "The Snows of Kilimanjaro" with the "poor Scott Fitzgerald" reference:

> I feel that I must tell you something which at first seemed better to leave alone: I wrote E about that story of his, asking him in the most measured terms not to use my name in future pieces of fiction. He wrote me back a crazy letter, telling me about what a great Writer he was and how much he loved his children. . . . To have answered it would have been like fooling with a lit firecracker.
>
> Some how I love that man, no matter what he says or does, but just one more crack and I think I would have to throw my weight with the gang and lay him. No one could hurt him in his first books but he has completely lost his head and the duller he gets about it, the more he is like a punch-drunk pug fighting himself in the movies. (Turnbull, 267, and see notes on 272 and 276).

The confusion about the dialogue in the August, 1936 *Esquire* version of "The Snows of Kilimanjaro" ("The rich are different from you and me . . . Yes they have more money."), which Hemingway uses to make Fitzgerald appear a gullible romantic, is interesting. According to Maxwell Perkins, at the actual event that generated the line, it is Hemingway who announced that he was getting to know the rich, and the critic, Mary Colum, who retorted that the only difference was that the rich had more money. (See Bruccoli, *Epic Grandeur*, 412). In the published book version of the story, "Scott Fitzgerald" was changed to "Julian," and Hemingway continued to hold the upper hand in his rivalry with "poor Scott."

Letter to Beatrice Dance about "Snows" (September 15, 1936):

> Too often literary men allow themselves to get into internecine quarrels and finish about as victoriously as most of the nations at the end of WWI. I consider it an example of approaching maturity on my part and am proud of my self control. He is quite as nervously broken down as I am but it manifests itself in different ways. His inclination is toward megalomania and mine toward melancholy. (Turnbull, 543).

Letter to Max Perkins about the Max Eastman affair (September 3, 1937):

> He (EH) is living at the present in a world so entirely his own that it is impossible to help him, even if I felt close to him at the moment, which I don't. I like him so much, though, that I wince when anything happens to him . . . you would think that a man who has arrived at the position of being practically his country's most eminent writer could be spared that yelping. (Turnbull, 275).

Although he congratulated Hemingway on the success of *For Whom the Bell Tolls*, in his Notebook Fitzgerald calls it "a thoroughly superficial book which has all the profundity of Rebecca." (Bruccoli, *Epic Grandeur*, 488).

In the essay "My Generation," Fitzgerald calls Wolfe's early death a "grievous loss. With Hemingway, Dos Passos, Wilder and Faulkner, he was one of a group of talents for fiction as rarely appears in a single hatching." (Cited in Andrew Turnbull, *Thomas Wolfe: A Biography*, 277).

In a letter (1940), Fitzgerald implied that he "had anticipated Faulkner in discovering the literary uses of the South. . . . It is a grotesquely pictorial country as I found out long ago, and as Mr. Falkner [*sic*] has since abundantly demonstrated." (Cited in Bruccoli, *Epic Grandeur*, 110).

––––––––

Attributing Hemingway's success as a writer to his having mastered and never varied from his method, Faulkner, while addressing a group of students at The University of Virginia in 1957, observed—in one of his rare references to Fitzgerald: "Too many tragically write themselves out too young. . . . That happened with Fitzgerald, happened with Sherwood Anderson, and so they go to pieces. . . ." [*Faulkner in the University*, 149–150].

John Dos Passos (1896–1970)

A Harvard-educated pacifist, Dos Passos ironically served, like the more enthusiastically militant Hemingway, with an ambulance unit in Italy. Lacking proof, each nevertheless insisted years later that they had met along the battlefront. They did undeniably meet in Paris in 1924 and shared the excitements of the fiesta at Pamplona.

Dos Passos and Hemingway also loved the same woman, albeit at different times. Katy Smith spent her summers in northern Michigan where her brother Bill was Hemingway's closest friend. When Hemingway returned from the war he lived briefly with Y. K. Smith, an older, married brother, and pursued Katy (among others) until she introduced him to her friend, Hadley, who became—after insisting that Hemingway stop his pursuit of Katy—the first Mrs. Hemingway.

Dos Passos met Katy some years later and married her in 1929—not long after Hemingway divorced Hadley.

As with so many others, Faulkner admired Dos Passos's early work but had little personal contact with him.

———

About *In Our Time*:

> *In Our Time* was out and I was trumpeting it abroad. My story was that basing his wiry short sentence on cablese [eds. "cablese"] and the King James Bible, Hemingway would become the first great American stylist. (John Dos Passos, *The Best Time: An Informal Memoir*, 142).

About *The Torrents of Spring:*

> I never did understand what Hem was up to in *The Torrents of Spring*. Was he deliberately writing stuff that Liveright . . . couldn't possibly print, or was it just a heartless boy's prank . . . I said it wasn't good enough to stand on its own feet as parody, and that *In Our Time* had been so damn good he ought to wait until he had something smashing to follow it with. (*The Best Time*, 157–8).

About *The Sun Also Rises*:

> Since reading the novel, I'm not quite sure which remembered events Hem made up and which actually happened. It was like a Cook's conducted tour with Hem as master of ceremonies. . . . (*The Best Time*, 154).

———

The people who served as models for Jake Barnes's supporting cast in *The Sun Also Rises* (Dos Passos was not one of them) boasted certain recall of the events at the San Fermin Festival in 1925—but their versions differed radically. However distorted Hemingway's portraits—some playful, some cruel—he wrote as a novelist, not as a reporter. The real people in his roman à clef have receded into obscurity; their fictional caricatures remain alive. (See Harold Loeb, *The Way it Was;* Bertram D. Sarason, *Hemingway and the Sun Set;* and especially Michael Reynolds's *Hemingway: The Paris Years,* 297–307).

Also alive, unfortunately, is his image of the sorry Robert Cohn—a character whose pitiable shortcomings seem as much a product of his Jewishness as of any of his actions. Which raises the question of anti-Semitism—a charge that has hovered like a withheld indictment over many writers of the Hemingway-Faulkner generation. The majority of the dominant Protestant class from which these writers came inherited—almost as a birthright—what they blithely, and (at the least) insensitively, regarded as a kind of genteel anti-Semitic prejudice. In some, like Mencken, Pound, Eliot, Wharton, and Wolfe, it could be virulent; in some of the others, it might appear as an occasional nervous tic—but in every instance, it was anti-Semitism and it was wrong.

Hemingway had Jewish friends, among them Nathan Asch, Isidor Schneider, Gertrude Stein, Alice Toklas, Harold Loeb, and Dorothy Parker, but not a single friendship endured. But then neither did his warm relationships with Dos Passos, Fitzgerald, or Donald Ogden Stewart. Hemingway often lent his hand in friendship but just as often withdrew it, and being Hemingway, did so at operatic volume and often in guttersnipe language.

Although Jason Compson's anti-Semitism in Faulkner's *The Sound and the Fury* is a component in his own bitter paranoia, the distinction between author's and character's perception is much blurrier in the portrayal of the Jewish fliers in "Death Drag" and, most grotesquely, in the figure of Colonel Feinman in *Pylon.* Faulkner was also

comfortable with stereotypic attitudes toward Jews in his correspondence. After *Flags in the Dust* was rejected as unpublishable, effectively severing Faulkner's contract with Liveright, Faulkner wrote his
aunt: "I'm going to be published by white folks now. Harcourt Brace
and Co. bought me from Liveright. Much, much nicer here." (October 1928, *Selected Letters*, 40–41).

But when Faulkner learned that Robert Haas's son had been killed
in the Pacific, he wrote to his stepson: " Mr. Robert Haas is vice presi-
dent of Random House. They publish my books. During the times
when I would be broke, year after year sometimes, I had only to write
to him and he would send me money—no hope to get it back, unless
I wrote another book. He's a Jew.

"He had an only son, and a daughter. In '40, the son withdrew
from Yale and became a Navy pilot. In '41, the girl about 20, joined
that Women's Ferry Squadron, is now flying . . . The boy was flying
torpedo planes off carriers . . . in the Pacific. He was killed last week.
The girl is still flying. All Jews. I just hope I don't run into some hundred percent American Legionnaire until I feel better." (Blotner, *Letters*, 175).

About *A Farewell to Arms*:

There's always been more ennui than action in war. It took years
and the reading of *La Chartreuse de Parme* and of Hemingway's
lovely description of the city in *A Farewell to Arms* before I
learned to appreciate Milan. (*The Best Time*, 61).

Letter to Hemingway (February, 1932):

The Bullfight book [*Death in the Afternoon*]—is absolutely the
best thing done on the subject—I mean all the description and

the dope—It seems to me an absolute model for how that sort of thing ought to be done—And all the accounts of individual fighters towns etc., are knockouts. I'm only doubtful . . . about the parts where Old Hem straps on the longwhite whiskers and gives the boys the lowdown . . . a book ought to be judged by the author according to the excellence of the stuff cut out. . . . (*The Fourteenth Chronicle: Letters and Diaries of John Dos Passos*, ed. Townsend Ludington, 402–03).

Letter to Hemingway (June 7, 1932):

. . . It sure makes me feel uneasy to hear you've been taking my advice about plucking some of the long white whiskers out of the end of *Death in the Afternoon*. . . . It's the God damndest best piece of writing that's seen the light for many a day on this continent. (*Fourteenth Chronicle*, 409–10).

The friendship between Hemingway and Dos Passos—warm and intimate for over a dozen years—frayed and ultimately tore apart in 1937 during the Spanish Civil War while they were working together on the documentary film, *The Spanish Earth*. Jose Robles, Dos Passos's close friend and translator, had been tried, convicted, and executed by the Spanish War Ministry as a Fascist spy in Valencia. Dos Passos was convinced that the killing was engineered by the Russian Stalinists as part of their determination to purge the socialist and anarchist elements among the Spanish Loyalists. Claiming information from high official sources, Hemingway argued otherwise. In retrospect, it seems clear that Dos Passos was right and that Robles was executed because he knew too much about the Kremlin's dominance over the Spanish War Ministry and wasn't considered by them as politically reliable. (See *Fourteenth Chronicle*, 495–97. See also Daniel Aaron, *Writers on the Left,* 343–53, Reynolds, *Hemingway: The 1930s,* 273–74, and Josephine Herbst, *The Parched Blue Sky of Spain,* 153–57).

Letter to Edmund Wilson (July 19, 1950) about *Across the River and Into the Trees:*

> How can a man in his senses leave such bullshit on the page? Everybody . . . writes acres of bullshit but people usually cross it out . . . *Intruder in the Dust* made me feel better. (*Fourteenth Chronicle,* 591).

Letter to Edmund Wilson (Aug. 1, 1950) about *Intruder in the Dust:*

> What do you think of *Intruder in the Dust?* I was very much set up by it. It's such a pleasure to find an American writer that passes middle age without going to pot. (*Fourteenth Chronicle,* 592).

Letter to Myra Champion (November 22, 1951):

> Unfortunately I only met Thomas Wolfe once, at Max Perkins' for dinner. We walked around New York . . . afterwards and wound up drinking coffee . . . somewhere. I forget what we talked about. As Hemingway said it was like being with a gigantic baby. There was a mild ferocity about his attitude that was very appealing. . . . (*Fourteenth Chronicle,* 597–98).

[1968]:

> Ernest and I used to read the Bible to each other. He began it. We read separate little scenes. From Kings, Chronicles. We didn't make anything out of it—the reading—but Ernest at that time [early 1920s] talked a lot about style. He was crazy about Ste-

phen Crane's "The Blue Hotel." It affected him very much. I was very much taken with him. He took me around to Gertrude Stein's. I wasn't quite at home there. A Buddha sitting up there surveying us. Ernest was much less noisy then than he was in later life. He felt such people were instructive. ("John Dos Passos," *Writers at Work: The Paris Review Interviews, Fourth Series*, ed. George Plimpton, 76).

I read a certain amount of Faulkner, and I'm very, very fond of some of his writing. "The Bear" and *As I Lay Dying*. "The Bear" is a marvelous hunting story. I liked *Intruder in the Dust*. He reminds me very much of the old storytellers I used to listen to down here [Virginia] when I visited summers as a boy. . . . I suppose what I like best in Faulkner is the detail. He is a remarkably accurate observer and builds his narratives—-which sometimes strike me as turgid—out of the marvelous raw material of what he has seen. (Plimpton, 87).

Letter to Joseph Blotner (October 7, 1969):

There's just a chance that I was introduced to Faulkner for a moment in New Orleans sometime in the mid twenties winter 1924? By either Sherwood Anderson or Lyle Saxon. My first real conversation with him was at the Hotel Algonquin . . . There were certainly other meetings but I don't remember them clearly. Then we met at . . . the National Academy on the occasion of the gold medal (awarded to Dos Passos) . . . after a good deal more wordage we finally got to our little act . . . Faulkner abandoned what he had to say, shoved the medal into my hand and said "Nobody ever deserved it more or had to wait for it longer." (*Fourteenth Chronicle*, 636).

The business about indebtedness I don't go for. I read *Pylon* with great pleasure about the time it came out, but I swear I don't think Faulkner was indebted to my work in any way. At certain times styles and methods are in the air, as contagious as the common cold. In that way we are all indebted to each other. (*Fourteenth Chronicle*, 636–37).

Archibald MacLeish (1892–1982)

A Yale graduate, MacLeish forsook law for poetry, came to Paris, and soon became another of Hemingway's friends. It was he in fact who took Hemingway to the American Hospital in Neuilly after a skylight fell on Hemingway's head. Their friendship survived a nasty imbroglio aboard the *Pilar* in the mid-30s. MacLeish, who most memorably proclaimed that "A poem should not mean / But be," went on to win the Pulitzer Prize for his epic poem, *Conquistador,* became Librarian of Congress, Assistant Secretary of State, and, later, the Boylston Professor of Rhetoric at Harvard.

Letter to John Peale Bishop (February 3, 1926):

> . . . Hemingway has just gone through on his way home to murder Messers Boni & Liveright. It seems they have turned down a satire of his [eds. *The Torrents of Spring*] on Anderson and there is great to do. I was out of town when he went through but found bear claw marks all over the front door. (*Letters of Archibald MacLeish*, ed. R. H. Winnick, 176).

Letter to Hemingway, after reading a carbon copy of *The Sun* manuscript (June, 1926):

> Jake stays with me. So does Ashley. So do bulls. . . . My one criticism is the one I gave you . . . that the novel is less of a block

than your best stories are. But I don't see how it can help but be a success, both d'estime and d'argent. It has got the one rare thing—common life. (Winnick, 179).

Letter to Hemingway (February 20, 1927):

I have never before seen a single story of yours I didn't like. Of course I admit to degrees— . . . all the way from a great story like the Killers . . . down to Mr and Mrs Elliott. . . . But the Pursuit Race took me all wrong. . . . I thought the first paragraph sounded like a parody of your stuff . . . and I thought the story itself missed fire. . . . (Winnick, 198–99).

Letter to Wyndham Lewis (December 8, 1927):

As for Ernest—your criticism was just. His stuff has a sensationalist base which I think he would concede and support intellectually. For me he is a true stylist (taught, curiously enough, pretty largely by G. Stein (in conversation) if you will believe his assertion!!) whose future is only limited by his willingness to seize it. . . . (Winnick, 210).

Letter to Hemingway on reading *A Farewell to Arms* (September 1, 1929):

What has happened is that you have mastered the self-imposed problems of your technique. There was a time when I wondered whether the restrained and tense understatement of your prose would not limit you to a certain kind of material. Now no one can wonder about that. The world of this book is a complete world, a world of emotion as well as of feeling . . . You become in one book the great novelist of our time. (Winnick, 230).

Letter to Hemingway (c. June 1, 1932):

> Max [Perkins] and I talked about the book [*Death in the After-noon*] and he thinks it is the best thing you have done. He is crazy about it. So is Dos . . . crazy about it. (Winnick, 251).

Letter to Ilona Karmel (July, 1951):

> Why is it that those who imitate Hemingway imitate his world as well as his rhythm and those who imitate Faulkner go down into Faulkner? . . . . Poetry is a way of entering the world. Which means that poetry is an action by which one man enters the world which is his world. (Winnick, 353).

(Summer, 1974):

> Hemingway and I were friends—close friends . . . from '24 or '25 until along in the thirties. Dos was a close friend always. So was John Peale Bishop. But these were . . . human friendships, friend-ships between men, not literary friendships. Reading Scott Fitz-gerald's letters to Ernest is illuminating in this connection: you see at once what was wrong with that friendship. Scott writes as a writer. And in friendship . . . there is no such thing as a writer: there is merely a man who sometimes writes. I can't imagine anything shallower than a friendship based on a common inter-est in the production of literature. Look at those letters of Scott's! They throw light on Scott's novels, sure, but on the rela-tion of two remarkable men? . . . ("Archibald MacLeish," *Writ-ers at Work: The Paris Review Interviews, Fifth Series*, ed. George Plimpton, 34).

> To be young in a time like that was incredible luck—to be young and in Paris. . . . Hemingway's *In Our Time* was the first solid

American proof to appear on the Seine—proof that a master of
English prose had established himself and that this master was
indubitably American. American not only by blood but by eye
and ear. (Plimpton, 39).

Robert McAlmon (1896–1956)

South Dakotan by birth, co-creator in Greenwich Village with William Carlos Williams of the magazine *Contact,* one of the earliest little
magazines, and one of the earliest of the expatriates in Paris where he
founded *Contact Editions*, which published early work by Hemingway, Stein, Pound, and others. McAlmon was married briefly to Winifred Ellerman, better known as Bryher, heiress to a British shipping
fortune as well as author of *Development*, an autobiographical novel
boasting an introduction by Amy Lowell, and lover of H.D. (Hilda
Doolittle, see below).

––––––––

[1923]:

Hemingway was a type not easy to size up. At times he was deliberately hard-boiled and case hardened; again he appeared deliberately innocent, sentimental, the hurt, but fairly sensitive
boy, wanting to be brave, not bitter or cynical but being somewhat both. . . . He approached a café with a small-boy, tough-
guy swagger . . . a potential snarl of scorn on his large-lipped,
rather loose mouth. (Robert McAlmon, *Being Geniuses Together.* Cited in *McAlmon and the Lost Generation*, ed. Robert
E. Knoll, 226–27).

[1923]:

> It is difficult to say who started the attitude in writing which occurs in 'My Old Man' and much present American work. It is not so much a style or an approach as an emotional attitude; that of an older person who insists upon trying to think and write as a child, and children in my experience are much colder and more ruthless in their observations. . . . Hemingway and a number of others have written in that, to me, falsely naïve manner . . . the hurt-child-being-brave tone is there, and all conversation is reduced to lone words or staccato phrases. (*Being Geniuses Together*, cited in Knoll, 227–28).

[1925]—About "Hills Like White Elephants":

> I didn't see the point of the story and reread it and encountered the phrase, 'Let the air in.' Later Hemingway informed me that my remark suggested the story. (*Being Geniuses Together*, cited in Knoll, 229).

[1925]:

> . . . on the way to Madrid, our train stopped at a wayside station. . . . On the track beside us was a flat car, upon which lay the maggot-eaten corpse of a dog. I . . . looked away, but Hemingway gave a dissertation on facing reality. It seems that he had seen the stacked corpses of men maggot-eaten in the war in a similar way. He advised a detached and scientific attitude toward the corpse of the dog. He tenderly explained that we of our generation must inure ourselves to the sight of pain and grim reality. . . . Ezra Pound had talked once of Hemingway's 'self-hardening

process.' (*Being Geniuses Together,* cited in Knoll, 230; William Carlos Williams tells the same story in his *Autobiography*).

Isidor Schneider (1896–1977)

Poet, critic, and novelist, Schneider was the publicity director at Boni and Liveright with whom Hemingway published *In Our Time* (1925). On receiving the manuscript of *The Torrents of Spring* (which Hemingway claimed to have written in six days), Liveright rejected it, saying that he was "patiently awaiting" *The Sun Also Rises*. He wrote Hemingway that he found *Torrents* a "bitter . . . and vicious caricature" of Sherwood Anderson (who was a prize Liveright author) and far too "cerebral" to attract readers. This effectively allowed Hemingway to break his contractual obligation to Liveright, enabling him to begin his lifelong connection with Charles Scribner and Sons (as it was then called) and Maxwell Perkins.

About *Torrents of Spring*:

> . . . I prefer any one of the In Our Time stories . . . I would not have gone all the way through if it were not your book. It seems to me to be too faithful to your subject. In spots it was actually as dull as Anderson. It was a good job but it became too elaborate. I'm expecting very different things from Sun Also Rises. I'm expecting it to be one of the biggest things done in America. (Unpublished letter in JFK Library).

Letter to EH (November, 1926) about *The Sun Also Rises*:

> It seems like a year since I've written to you. I have sat down often to write but couldn't make up my mind to tell you what I

wanted to tell you . . . I don't like *The Sun Also Rises*. . . . At the bottom I think it is because we like different things and agree only in that we both want to be honest about them.

I don't like the trick of the plot . . . the love of the unsexed man for a loose-sexed woman . . . neither tragedy nor comedy for me. I never got to believe in it. . . . I couldn't like or dislike the people. . . . I just don't care about them, except the bull fighter. . . . The only action in the book I liked was the Fiesta. That had a sort of horrible interest for me, like a report of a dissection. . . .

I felt so worked up about it that I wrote a piece on it and sent it to the *Saturday Review*. They rejected it—and I'm glad they did. I felt too many fine things gone to waste in your book, and I was afraid no reviewer would see. I was right . . . I thought it would be good for somebody to come out against it. . . . (Unpublished letter, JFK Library).

In an unpublished letter to Schneider (Jan., 1927), Hemingway responded at length to Schneider's criticisms, acknowledging that his characters were "hollow and dull" because "that is the way they are." Hemingway also thanked Schneider for not publishing an unfavorable review. Eight years later (August 19, 1935), Hemingway wrote bitterly to the Soviet critic Ivan Kashkeen about Schneider and other left-wing critics, complaining that their political orthodoxy prevented literary insight. (See Baker, *Letters*, 417–18).

Letter to EH (March 8, 1927) about "The Killers":

The Killers is a wonderful story. I feel about it that it is one of the best stories I have ever read. (Unpublished letter, JFK Library).

Sylvia Beach (1887–1962)

An American expatriate from New Jersey, Beach opened the book-store, Shakespeare and Company, in 1919, published Joyce's *Ulysses* in 1922, and served as Paris den mother for young writers until 1941. She encouraged them—Hemingway, Pound, Eliot, Wilder, and Mac-Leish among others—to gather at her shop to browse, borrow books, talk, and to solicit her always accessible sympathy.

Hemingway's genuine affection for Beach was undisturbed by her well-known lesbian relationship with Adrienne Monnier. Similarly, until he turned on Stein in the late 1920s, he had no difficulty in re-garding Stein-Toklas as a couple with whom he was completely com-fortable. Clearly, not only did he find lesbians unthreatening, but, on the basis of *The Garden of Eden*, more than a little fascinating. This contrasts sharply with his general homophobia, witness, for example, his strong aversion to Glenway Wescott, the probable model for Rob-ert Prentiss in *The Sun Also Rises*, whom he refers to in a letter to Ezra Pound as "the fairies [*sic*] best bet in literature." (cited in Gerry Brenner, *A Comprehensive Companion to Hemingway's "A Moveable Feast*," 261).

A glancing light on this complex situation may be inferred from Truman Capote's loathing of Hemingway and his work. When Nel-son Algren's novel, *The Man with the Golden Arm* (1949) appeared, Hemingway submitted this blurb: "All you Capote fans, get your hats and get your coats, here comes a real writer." In *Conversations*, Capote countered with what were among the earliest public ques-tionings of Hemingway's masculinity: "I don't think anything Hemingway did was one of the best of anything. There was a mean man. . . . [H] was a closet everything. . . . I think that he was enor-mously vulnerable and sensitive in a way that I never thought of being. I'm sensitive about other people, but I'm not sensitive about

myself." (*Conversations with Capote*, Lawrence Grobel (93–94).
Among the many commentaries on Hemingway's attitude on gender preference, one of the more thorough is Carl P. Eby, *Hemingway's Fetishism*, 1999.

Faulkner, on the other hand, seems to have been either more toler-
ant or, more likely, simply indifferent about such relationships, admiring during the 1920s such homosexual friends as his fellow
Mississippian, the novelist Stark Young, and William Spratling, the
craftsman and designer with whom he roomed in New Orleans.
About women, however, Faulkner appeared to have had significant
sexual fixations, as he himself inadvertently demonstrates in his letter
praising Anita Loos's *Gentlemen Prefer Blondes* (1925): "I have just
read the Blonde book . . . Please accept my envious congratulations
on Dorothy . . . I am still rather Victorian in my prejudices regarding
the intelligence of women, despite Elinor Wylie and Willa Cather and
all the balance of them. But I wish I had thought of Dorothy first."
(February, 1926), Blotner, *Letters*, 32. Frederick Karl argues strongly
that Faulkner instinctively divided all women into two classes: whore
or madonna (*Faulkner*, 211). But homosexuality and lesbianism
seemed not to figure markedly as issues in his psychic landscape.

[1921]:

> A customer we liked . . . was that young man you saw almost
> every morning over there in a corner at Shakepeare & Company,
> reading the magazines or Captain Marryat or some other book.
> . . . My 'best customer' he called himself. . . . I felt the warmest
> friendship for Ernest Hemingway from the day we met. (Sylvia
> Beach, *Shakespeare and Company*, 77).
>
> Hemingway was a great pal of Joyce's and Joyce remarked to
> me . . . that he thought it was a mistake, Hemingway's thinking

himself such a tough fellow and McAlmon trying to pass himself off as a sensitive type. It was the other way round. . . .
(Beach, 78).

[1936]:

Readings at Shakespeare and Company: Ernest Hemingway for
once made an exception to his rule against reading in public and
consented to appear if Stephen Spender could be persuaded to
join him. So we had a double reading, and a great sensation it
made! (Beach, 214).

[1945]:

There was still a lot of shooting going on . . . when a string of
jeeps came up the street and stopped in front of my house. I
heard a deep voice calling "Sylvia."

    "It's Hemingway! It's Hemingway!" cried Adrienne [Mon-
nier, Beach's companion]. I flew downstairs; we met with a
crash; he picked me up and swung me around and kissed me
while people on the street and in the windows cheered. . . .
(Beach, 223).

Conrad Aiken (1889–1973)

No evidence indicates that Aiken ever met Hemingway, but Faulkner
from his youth onward praised his fellow Southerner's poetry—"a
rift of heaven sent blue" and admired him above the "entire yelping
pack" (especially Sandburg, Lindsay, and Kreymborg). (See Blotner,
Faulkner, A Biography 1, 300).

Review of *The Sun Also Rises* (*New York Herald Tribune Books*, October 31, 1926):

> The dialogue is brilliant. If there is better dialogue being written today I do not know where to find it. It is alive with the rhythms and idioms, the pauses and suspensions and innuendoes and shorthands, of living speech. (Cited in Audre Hanneman, *Ernest Hemingway: A Comprehensive Bibliography*, 350).

On Faulkner in *The Atlantic Monthly*, November, 1939:

> What sets him above—shall we say it firmly—all his American contemporaries, is his continuous preoccupation with the novel as *form*, his passionate concern with it, and a degree of success with it which would have clearly commanded the interest and respect of Henry James himself (Quoted in Blotner, *Faulkner, A Biography* 2, 1032).

Harry Crosby (1898–1929)

A wealthy Bostonian, Harvard-educated, and, like Hemingway and Cummings, an ambulance driver during World War I, Crosby was also a death-obsessed drunkard whose weird poems and dreams fascinated his fellow expatriates. To better purpose, however, he and his wife, Caresse, established the Black Sun Press which published major pieces by Joyce and D. H. Lawrence, and encouraged Hart Crane to finish "The Bridge." He met Hemingway on a skiing trip at Gstaad in 1926, and they attended horse races together at Auteuil and ran with the bulls at Pamplona. Crosby shot and killed a girlfriend, Josephine Bigelow, at the Hotel des Artistes in New York, then committed suicide. At Caresse's request, Archibald MacLeish kept a deathwatch over his corpse at Bellevue Hospital. Crosby was thirty-one. (See Geoffrey Wolff, *Black Sun*, 288).

(December 28, 1926):

> H[emingway] the realist and M[acLeish] the dreamer. . . . And they both know Joyce and go to his readings. . . . And they both think Cocteau is an ass and so do I and all three of us despise the English. And M said to read Anabase [a poem by St. John Perse, translated by T. S. Eliot, 1924] and H said he wrote the story about the Wind Blows ["The Three-Day Blow"] (the best story in the book) in half an hour. And M is quieter but they both have charm. . . . And M said he read very little. And H had been to the cock-fighting in Seville. And we drank. And H could drink us under the table. And everyone wanted to pay for the wine. And M won (that is he paid). (From *Shadows of the Sun*, cited in Geoffrey Wolff, *Black Sun: The Brief Transit and Violent Eclipse of Harry Crosby*, 182).

An anecdote that Katherine Anne Porter told and retold in several versions relates that Elinor Wylie rang her doorbell (or telephoned her) early one morning (or late at night) in a frenzied state. (Sara Teasdale observed that Wylie, the poet/novelist whose beauty was legendary in Greenwich Village, seemed heroic if you liked her; hysterical if you didn't.) Wylie announced to Katherine Anne that she was going to kill herself and the only person in the world that she cared to say good-bye to was Katherine. "Well, that's sweet of you to think of me," Katherine said she replied. "Good-bye." And she shut the door (or hung up the phone.) Wylie evidently survived the encounter—if not the anecdote—dying of a stroke at the premature age of 44.

The story is undoubtedly a major embellishment on whatever kernel of truth may have been its origin, but it is symptomatic of something larger and more serious. From January 19, 1919, when the twin sister/poets, Gladys and Dorothea Cromwell, committed suicide on their return Atlantic crossing from France after serving in the Red Cross, to January, 1933, when Teasdale downed a handful of sleeping pills and drowned quietly in her bathtub at One Fifth Avenue, these dozen or so years scythed a significant swathe of self-inflicted deaths on the members of this generation. Because of his social prominence and the tabloid circumstances of his performance, Harry Crosby's immolation received a good deal of notice. And Hart Crane's exit from the stern of the *Orizaba* en route from Veracruz to New York in 1932 is memorable largely for the ellipsis that marked the end of a potentially masterful career. Less noted at about the same time was the death of Vachel Lindsay—for a brief period, the most popular poet in America—who swallowed a bottle of Lysol in what must have been an exceptionally painful way to die. Statistically, the proportion of suicides in this period may not have been significantly different from other years, but the shock of these events and the notoriety of the participants must surely have given suicide a heightened presence within the artistic community.

As we have mentioned elsewhere, the post-World War I era facilitated radical changes in the traditional structures of American life, and these changes tended to be articulated most extremely by artists on the cutting edge of the times. The abrupt loosening of social, religious, and sexual strictures presented our poets and novelists with an extraordinary freedom to experiment with their lives in a way which was totally new. As evidenced by the broken marriages, nervous breakdowns, massive depressions, and rampant alcoholism, many of these authors found themselves liberated into cyclonic orbits with no return, unmoored, and without internal or external restraints on their behavior. And to the degree that they harbored unrealistic ambitions of securing artistic success and personal happiness, their perceptions of failure could lead to intolerable pain and, in the last resort, self-inflicted death.

With his horrendous family history of black depressions and suicide (father, brother, sister), Hemingway might be expected to be insightful, if not empathetic, on the subject. His position, however, was clear, oft-repeated, and unyielding. Suicide was the coward's option. Central to the code of bravery he espoused was the imperative to refuse to succumb to ultimate despair even when—or especially when— one "cannot resign" oneself. In fact, an unflinching confrontation with death is the thematic key to much of his work and one of the major sources of its infectious popularity. Consequently, his suicide—and all suicides are ultimately inexplicable—casts a dark retroactive shadow on his fiction, on his life, and, indirectly, the accomplishments of his entire generation.

In the figure of Quentin Compson in 1929, on the other hand, Faulkner captured the unraveling consciousness of a suicide-on-the-brink more vividly perhaps than anyone has ever done. Acquainted with grief in a directly personal way—the heartbreaking death of his nine-day-old daughter, Alabama, in 1931 and the 1935 airplane crash which killed his brother Dean—Faulkner's stern response is grimly positive. In the words he gives Harry Wilbourne in *The Wild Palms* (1939), "Between grief and nothing I will take grief," he just barely manages a courageous grip on the slipperiest edge of the abyss.

Edmund Wilson (1895–1972)

Wilson, a classmate of Fitzgerald's at Princeton, first encountered Hemingway by mail. As yet scarce noticed, Hemingway wrote from

Toronto in November, 1923, thanking Wilson for reading *Three Stories and Ten Poems* and calling it to the attention of the *New York Tribune*'s literary editor. A year later, Hemingway wrote again, grateful once more to Wilson for a review of the work in *Dial*. (see below). They met in New York in 1924 and Wilson became one of the rare critics Hemingway admired, until admiration turned to antagonism—see commentary below.

Faulkner and Wilson met on the printed page as young contributors to the distinguished New Orleans literary magazine *Double Dealer* in 1925. Whether they ever met in person is uncertain, but Faulkner made clear in one of his discussions at the University of Virginia in 1957 that he separated himself as a "writer" from "literary" men like Edmund Wilson (overlooking the fact, perhaps, that Wilson had published two fairly successful novels and thought of himself as a serious playwright).

Letter to Alyse Gregory at the *Dial* magazine (September 4, 1924):

> . . . I wish you would print my little notice of Hemingway's books sometime soon, if you are able to, so that he can get the benefit of it. . . . (*Edmund Wilson: Letters on Literature and Politics*, ed. Elena Wilson, 14).

About *In Our Time* in the *Dial* (October, 1924):

> [Hemingway is] the only American writer but one—Mr. Sherwood Anderson—who has felt the genius of Gertrude Stein's *Three Lives* and has evidently been influenced by it. Indeed, Miss Stein, Mr. Anderson and Mr. Hemingway may now be said to form a school by themselves. (Cited in James R. Mellow, *Charmed Circle: Gertrude Stein and Company*, 271).

Letter to Christian Gauss (February 23, 1926):

> Hemingway has been in town for a few days—has now gone back
> to France . . . Scribner's is going to publish Hemingway in the
> future. I read his book the other day and I thought it was awfully
> good. Did you tell me you didn't like his writings? I wish you
> would look into *In Our Time* some time. (*Letters,* 129).

Letter to Hemingway (January 7, 1927):

> I think your book [*The Sun Also Rises*] is a knockout—perhaps
> the best piece of fiction that any American of the new crop has
> done. (*Letters,* 140).

Letter to Hemingway (May 4, 1927):

> Your Italian sketches are fine. They have been received with en-
> thusiasm in the office and will appear this week, I think. I liked
> the stories in Scribner's very much, especially the one about the
> Italian major ["In Another Country"]. I like "The Killers" too,
> but I thought you gave the thugs a line of banter which sounded
> a little too much like the hero of your novel and his friend on
> their fishing trip—that is to say, a little too sophisticated. (*Let-
> ters,* 140).

At this time, Hemingway was far less prickly about criticism than he
would become. In a letter to Perkins (December 1, 1930), he wrote: "I
hope you will tell Wilson that he is the only critic for whose writing I
have any respect, but that I believe he is sometimes . . . wrong. . . . If
I disagree with him about the 'romantic' ending of 'Farewell to Arms'
it does not mean that I think him an ass, but that possibly I've seen
more people die than he has and that we differ in our attitude toward

the pleasure of sexual intercourse. I'm not in the least angry at Wilson who has a right to put in anything he wants. . . . " (*The Only Thing that Counts: The Ernest Hemingway/Maxwell Perkins Correspondence, 1925—1947*, ed. Matthew J. Bruccoli, 151).]

Letter to Allen Tate (July 20, 1931):

> As for the "coming generation," I tried to make clear that what I expected to happen was what in fact was already happening when I wrote [in *Axel's Castle*]: a combination of Symbolism and naturalism. Joyce had already effected this and all the people who stem from him . . . continue it: Expressionism, the later O'Neill, Dos Passos, the Dadaists in their later manifestations; Thomas Wolfe, I suppose; and your countryman William Faulkner is an example of that, isn't he? (*Letters*, 212).

Letter to Fitzgerald (November 7, 1932):

> I thought Hemingway's bullfighting book was pretty maudlin— the only thing of his I haven't liked. (*Letters*, 229).

Letter to Fitzgerald (March 26, 1933):

> I've sent back *Sanctuary* through *The New Republic*. I thought it was pretty good. He [Faulkner] certainly has a compelling imagination, and I thought the whole fable very well conceived, though sloppily executed stylistically and technically. (*Letters*, 229).

Letter to Fitzgerald (October 21, 1933):

> I have just read Hemingway's new stories [*Winner Take Nothing*], and though the best of them are excellent, now is your time to creep up on him. (*Letters*, 231).

Letter to Maxwell Perkins (June 11, 1935):

> Won't you send some of your new American books to Sergei
> Alimov, one of the most interesting of the Russian writers, who
> reads English and is contemplating a book on American litera-
> ture. . . . They have just gotten out a volume of selections from
> Hemingway, and are mad about him. Alimov is very much ex-
> cited over what I have told him about *The Green Hills of Af-
> rica*—do send him a copy when it is out. . . . I've been more than
> ever impressed by our contemporary writing since I've seen how
> the Russians are influenced by it. They seem to read it more than
> any other. (*Letters*, 272).

Letter to Malcolm Cowley (October 20, 1938):

> I was thinking a year ago that something must have gone very
> wrong with you when you could get yourself into a state of
> mind to praise Hemingway's Popeye-the-Sailor novel [*To Have
> and Have Not*]—though I am sure that your natural instincts
> must have told you that it was mostly lousy and actually repre-
> sented Hemingway in pieces! (*Letters*, 310. Wilson is referring
> to Cowley's review of October 20, 1937 in *The New Republic*).

Letter to Maxwell Perkins (October 25, 1938):

> Thanks for the Hemingway book. I didn't think much of the
> play [*The Fifth Column*], but the four new stories are wonderful.
> 'The Short Happy Life of Francis Macomber' is as good as the
> *Green Hills of Africa* was bad. (*Letters*, 313).

Letter to Florine Katz (March 7, 1941), referring to Scribner's recant-
ing on their contract with Wilson for *The Wound and the Bow*, subsequently published by Houghton Mifflin:

... when they [Scribner] laid eyes on my essay on Hemingway ["Hemingway: Gauge of Morale"], they protested that they could not print it ... —this in spite of the fact that the essay had appeared in *The Atlantic Monthly*, that Max Perkins had read it and knew it was to be included, that what it said was mainly favorable . . . , and that they had been genuinely enthusiastic about publishing it. Hemingway has been getting worse (crazier) of late years, and they are scared to death he may leave them. (*Letters*, 387).

Letter to Gertrude Stein [in reference to a Fitzgerald memorial volume], (April 17, 1942):

... he [Fitzgerald] was working on a book about Hollywood, which I believe would have been one of his best things. . . . He had been feeling rather happy about the progress he was making with his book. I think you are right: that he had the constructive gift that Hemingway doesn't have at all. . . . (*Letters*, 346).

By this time, Hemingway had included Wilson in his expanding list of bêtes noires as seen in his response to a suggestion that Wilson edit Fitzgerald's letters. Hemingway to Perkins (February 25, 1944):

Would suggest that John Peale Bishop edit the letters. John is unfailably [*sic*] kind, impersonal and disinterested while Wilson is usually twisting the facts to cover some expressed error of critical judgement he has made in the past or some prejudice or lack of knowledge or scholarship. He is also extremely dishonest . . . His criticism is like reading second rate gospels written by some one who is out on parole. He reads most interestingly on all the things one does not know about. On the things one knows about truly he is stupid, inaccurate, uninformative and pretentious. . . . He is the great false-honest, false-craftsman, falsegreat-critic of our exceedingly sorry times. . . . You can trace the moral decay of his criticism on a parrallel [*sic*] line with the decline in Dos Passos's writing through their increasing dishonesty about money and other things, mostly their being dominated by women. (Bruccoli, 329–30).

In spite of Wilson's several attempts at persuasion, Wilson's friend, Vladimir Nabokov (1899–1977), the Russian-American novelist, essayist, and lepidopterist was as adamant in his rejection of Faulkner as he was of Dostoevsky, whom he regarded as "a claptrap journalist and a slapdash comedian." Nabokov did, however, admire Hemingway for having "a voice of his own."

"Pushkin, Shakespeare and himself constitute his three favorite writers. Mann, Faulkner and André Gide receive the doubtful honor of being the three writers he most detests." (*Wellesley College News,* October 9, 1947. Cited in Brian Boyd, *Vladimir Nabokov: The American Years,* 122).

Dear Bunny [Wilson] (November 21, 1948),

I have carefully read Faulkner's Light in August . . . and it has in no way altered the low (to put it mildly) opinion I have of his work and other (innumerable) books in the same strain. I detest these puffs of stale romanticism . . . Faulkner's belated romanticism and quite impossible biblical rumblings and 'starkness' . . . and all the rest of the bombast seem to me . . . offensive . . . The book you sent me is one of the tritest and most tedious examples of a trite and tedious genre . . . imagine that this kind of thing (white trash, velvety Negroes, those bloodhounds out of Uncle Tom's Cabin melodramas, steadily baying through thousands of swampy books) may be necessary in a social sense, but it is not literature. . . . (*The Nabokov-Wilson Letters: 1940–1971*, ed. Simon Karlinsky, 213).

The long friendship between Wilson and Vladimir Nabokov soured shortly after the multilingual and prodigiously gifted Nabokov published in 1964 a four-volume translation of Alexander Pushkin's *Eugene Onegin* over which he had labored for almost fifteen years. Reviews were almost uniformly hostile, charging incompetence, dullness, and incomprehensibility, but what wounded Nabokov most was Wilson's suggestion (echoed, incidentally, by Robert Lowell) that his Russian was faulty. The exchanges between Wilson and Nabokov in the *New York Review of Books* and the *New York Times* grew increasingly testy, Nabokov citing Wilson's "muddleheaded and ill-informed" description of Russian prosody as evidence that he "remains organically incapable of reading," while Wilson responded that such petulance recalled Degas's retort to Whistler, "You behave as if you had no talent."

Letter to Arthur Mizener (March 3, 1950):

I don't believe, by the way, as you seem to, that Gertrude Stein's interest in him [Fitzgerald] was prompted solely by her pique against Hemingway. She was a very good judge of writing, and the only time I ever met her she talked about Scott with intelligence. She said—what is perfectly true—that he had much more sense of form than Hemingway. (*Letters*, 477).

Letter to John Dos Passos (September 5, 1950):

I was very much impressed by *Intruder in the Dust*—wasn't I telling you about it when it first came out? It is better if read in conjunction with the book *Go Down, Moses*, to which it is a sequel, and was written before Faulkner had gotten himself into a state of mind about the Civil Rights program and has less boy's adventure story in it. (*Letters*, 490).

Letter to Alfred Kazin (July 8, 1961):

I was somewhat upset by Hemingway's death. Of course he often made a fool of himself, but it is as if a whole corner of my generation had suddenly and horribly collapsed. I knew that the desperation in his stories was real, and his suicide—as evidently it was—makes his drinking and posing seem pathetic, because it must have been an effort to counteract and cover up the other thing. (*Letters*, 602).

Letter to Morley Callaghan (1962):

. . . I have just read *That Summer* [*That Summer in Paris: Memories of Tangled Friendships with Hemingway, Fitzgerald, and Some Others*], with, of course, intense interest. You have performed the feat—rare in the literary world—of writing about other writers truthfully and with understanding and yet without malice. You must be the first person—I haven't read the family memoirs—who has really told what Hemingway was like. You evidently got the benefit of the charming side of both him and Scott more than I ever did. I saw Hemingway—always on his visits to New York—probably not half a dozen times. . . . (*Letters*, 388).

Letter to Dos Passos (November 26, 1966):

I have just read *The Best Times* and very much enjoyed it. . . . Why didn't you tell about your experiences during the Spanish

War and the reasons—execution of Robles, etc.—for the cool-
ness between you and Hemingway?—all this, so far as I knew
about it, seemed so characteristic both of him and of you. (*Letters*, 665. See also Michael Reynolds, *Hemingway: the 1930's*,
273–74, and Josephine Herbst, *The Starched Blue Sky of Spain*,
150–55).

Letter to Alfred Kazin (April 18, 1969):

That was an excellent article on Dos Passos. . . . Corrections: The
writers of his generation you mention were not all, as you say,
'close friends.' Cummings knew Dos Passos because they had
been at Harvard together, but he did not know Scott Fitzgerald;
he could only barely have met Hemingway, if at all. I have just
got the Baker biography of Hemingway, however, and find that
Hemingway greatly admired *The Enormous Room* and 'introduced' Cummings to Sylvia Beach—whether personally is not
clear. (*Letters*, 699).

TWO

Sounds of the South

*W*ith at least three vibrant and supportive centers of literary activity after World War I (Richmond, Nashville, and New Orleans), Southern writers enjoyed a kind of communality and sense of shared heritage largely absent in the rest of the country. Partly triggered by the repercussions of the Scopes Trial in Dayton (1925), the notion of Southern exceptionalism became elevated to something close to an ideology. Accordingly, most Southern writers felt a sympathetic kinship with the general precepts suggested by the Fugitives at Vanderbilt (1922–25), which were later more emphatically set out in the Agrarian Manifesto, *I'll Take My Stand* (1930). At a time when the effects of massive immigration and large-scale industrialization were transforming much of the Northeast and Middle West, Southerners, in Donald Davidson's words, must embrace "the traditions of the South, bound up with the ways of land and people . . . as agrarian, conservative, stable, religious." "Regionalism," he asserted, "is not an end in itself, not a literary affectation, not an aesthetic credo, but a condition of literary realization. The function of a region is to endow the American artist with character and purpose." (*The Attack on Leviathan*, 1938, 93, 239).

Much of this perspective can be seen in the burst of literary activity displayed: in the plays of Paul Green; in the poetry of Merrill Moore, Allen Tate, John Crowe Ransom, and the younger Robert Penn

Warren; and in the fiction of Hamilton Basso, James Branch Cabell, Ellen Glasgow, Caroline Gordon, DuBose Heyward, Elizabeth Madox Roberts, and Stark Young. More intensely, perhaps, than writers in other parts of the country, Southerners expressed a sense of rootedness in a region and an awareness of local history as a vital presence in everyday life. It is also true that for many of them, their instinctive sympathy with "The Lost Cause" of the Confederacy and/or their consciousness of the indefensible racial relations within which they lived presented them with a host of ambiguities that had to affect their work.

Neither Hemingway nor Faulkner was immune to the disease of racism but their responses ran contrary to expected prescriptions. Few veterans of the Civil War were alive during Hemingway and Faulkner's adolescence. But those old soldiers, both the Blue and the Gray, had already, more than a half century later, passed on to their descendants a perverse and ugly legacy. Whether slavery had been, as Lincoln said, "a moral, a social, and a political wrong," was not at issue. Race was—and in Hemingway's Oak Park, Illinois and Faulkner's Oxford, Mississippi, society held in common a belief that black was inferior to white.

With an attitude similar to their casual anti-Semitism, the citizens of Oak Park, like many of their Northern neighbors, practiced what Michael Reynolds called "benign racism." Hemingway's father, a doctor, cared for native Indians without really caring about them. As Reynolds writes (*The Young Hemingway*, 163–64; 238–39), Hemingway, like his fellow residents, regarded himself as untainted. Indeed Hemingway registered shock when Hadley, his young wife, referred to Negroes as "nigs" despite using like expressions while retaining friendships with black Americans. Nowhere is there evidence of his participation in the early stages of the civil rights movement.

The complexity of Faulkner's involvement with race begins, we think, with Uncle Ned Barnett, an elderly black man who had served the family as a slave during the Civil War, who remembered, so he swore, the city ablaze. When the family moved to Oxford, Uncle Ned inherited his master's wardrobe, then wore it with elegance. He waited on tables, trained horses, milked cows (always wearing a tie). Once a slave, forever black, and now, a freed man who categorically denied any personal relevance of the Emancipation Proclamation. He was, he insisted, never freed because he just refused to be freed. (William Anderson, *The Southern Sentinel*, 19, July 1962. Cited in Blotner. 1. N. 29). What Uncle Ned had from the beginning was a powerful sense of self, a resolute dignity he would allow no man— white or black—to violate. It was such a man who laid the founda- tions for William Faulkner's own complex approach to race, despite his unabashed references to blacks as "coons" or "niggers."

Addressing his daughter's high school graduating class in 1951, Faulkner warned against using fear to rob one of individuality and urged the young to "believe in man's capacity for courage and endur- ance and sacrifice." (Blotner, 1386). With a stubbornness that would have delighted Uncle Ned but confused and irritated impatient devo- tees of immediate Federal civil rights' action, he refused to debate Dr. W. E. B. DuBois, arguing that the distinguished scholar and politician, however "right morally, legally, and ethically," could never persuade him to alter his own confidence in the "practicality" of "moderation and patience." (*Letters*, 398).

By the mid-1950s, Faulkner directed his pleas for moderation with growing impatience, but not as his supporters had expected. Segrega- tion was doomed, he continued to reason, but its sentence and execu- tion must lie in the hands, not of the Federal government, but of those who had suffered generations of segregation—The American Black. As the new agents of change—blacks would have to be, as he wrote to a black couple he had once employed, "*more* responsible, more honest, more moral, more industrious, more literate and educated." (*Letters*, 444). The black must, Faulkner concludes, attain a level at which whites will by choice not by law, be compelled to say, "Please come and be equal with us." (*Letters*, 444).

Under intensive questioning during sessions with university students and especially in an interview with the *New York Times*, Faulkner alienated most of a hitherto enthusiastic liberal contingent. What he had championed was an impossible, politically naive combination of commitment to equality by degrees and a stubborn, sullen hostility toward governmental interference. Much though he hoped to stay a middle course, Faulkner warned, he would if he had to "fight for Mississippi against the United States, even if it meant going out into the street and shooting Negroes."

Hemingway's relative indifference, Faulkner's passionate if unsatisfactory commitment to racial issues—to what extent did these affect their creativity in fiction? Only, we would suggest, insofar as they fired their imagination. Surely, Hemingway was moved by his youthful experiences among native Americans: the Indian who, agonized by his wife's screams during childbirth, commits suicide ("Indian Camp"); the Indian girl who first broke his heart ("Ten Indians"); the Indian who defied and humiliated his father ("The Doctor and the Doctor's Wife"). And among blacks, Bugs, the tough but almost maternal companion ("The Battler") who cares for his mad, punch-drunk white friend. Years later, on safari with his wife in Africa, he was infatuated with a young Wakamban girl, Debba, in his final posthumous novel (*True at First Light*).

In fiction, Ralph Ellison remarked in an interview, "stereotypes partake of archetypes . . . let's take Faulkner. When Lucas Beauchamp first appears . . . he appears as a stereotype (*Go Down, Moses*), but as he was developed throughout the successive novels (*Intruder in the Dust*), he became one of Faulkner's highest representatives of human quality." ("An Interview with Ralph Ellison," reprinted from *Ombra* in *Harper's Magazine*, March, 1967, 80–81). To what extent did Uncle Ned enter into Simon, a servant to Bayard Sartoris? How many details did Uncle Ned's female counterpart, Mammie Callie, contribute to the creation of the unforgettable Dilsey in *The Sound and the Fury*? She was in fact Caroline Barr, the house servant Faulkner knew from his childhood till her death in 1940 at the age of 100. Buried in a segregated area, the inscription on her tombstone, prepared by Faulkner, was dedicated to one "Who was born in slavery and who gave to my family a fidelity without stint or calculation of recompense and to my childhood an immeasurable devotion and love."

The characters in the fiction and the sullen racist menace that seethes in stories like "Dry September" and in *Light in August* are not, however, merely portraits drawn from and to life. Rather are they inventions that search beyond specificities, seeking some level of understanding that may lead us beyond racism, even, perhaps, encouraging us—of whatever color—to stand proudly one day beside Uncle Ned and Mammie Callie.

John Peale Bishop (1892–1944)

West Virginian by birth, poet, novelist, short story writer, and essayist by profession. Bishop attended Princeton with Edmund Wilson and F. Scott Fitzgerald, who drew upon him as a character in *This Side of Paradise* and whom he, in turn, memorialized in a sensitive elegy ("The Hours"). After service in France, he lingered for several years in Paris. Allen Tate and Archibald MacLeish were his closest friends.

Letter to Allen Tate (June 24, 1931). On the judgment of characters in literature:

> the treatment of Temple Drake [the protagonist of Faulkner's novel, *Sanctuary*] "is a form of judgment, cruel but essentially just. It is what should have happened to her. But, beyond the Swiftian rage, there is also in the book a purely personal resentment at her. The resentment is not pure. Nor is the judgment. . . .
>
> Hemingway, who has no historical sense, nevertheless manages to give a pretty sound judgment on his characters. Morally the man is simple but on the whole sound. He sticks to a few heroic virtues and is able to dispense with complexity. (*The Republic of Letters in America: The Correspondence of John Peale Bishop & Allen Tate*, eds. Thomas Daniel Young and John J. Hindle, 38–40 passim).

Letter from Allen Tate to Bishop (Jan. 12, 1941):

> She [Katherine Anne Porter] owes, she says, nothing to observation: by putting the observation so far back into her childhood she virtually claims to have invented it. She owed nothing to experience—just as Ernest used to owe nothing to any other writer. This is the last vanity of the artist; and I have never known a woman writer who has survived it. Ernest survives it by getting a new war and a new girl. (*Republic of Letters*, 173).

Although Hemingway was married four times (Hadley Richardson, Pauline Pfeiffer, Martha Gellhorn, and Mary Welsh) and had possible liaisons with Jane Mason, Adriana Ivancich, and Debba (*True At First Light*), in some sense he was a conventional, albeit, serial monogamist. Siring three sons, addressing most eligible women as "Daughter," and traveling extravagantly, it is difficult to ascribe a permanent home for him. (The Finca Vigia, where he lived longer than anywhere else, seems to have been a combination of retreat, launching pad, work-place, and sort of Club Caribbean for entertaining.)

Faulkner, on the other hand, who waited patiently for ten years until his childhood love, Estelle Oldham, was divorced so that he could marry her, seemed to have had no compunction about forming serious engagements with—among others—Helen Baird, Meta Carpenter, Else Johnson, Joan Williams, and Jean Stein; and this, while enduring a cruelly unsatisfactory marriage which he adamantly refused to dissolve. In one of his rare critical remarks about his rival, which highlights the deeply rooted differences between them, he said: "Hemingway's mistake was that he thought he had to marry all of them." (Blotner, 179). Curiously enough, just as Hemingway delighted in the sobriquet, "Papa," Faulkner enjoyed being called "Pappy." It seems clear that the traditional notions of home, hearth, and family—so ostentatiously displayed in Rowan Oak—were as unshakable and necessary to his deepest sense of self as they were unimaginable for Hemingway.

Evelyn Scott (1893–1963)

Born in Tennessee, educated in New Orleans, in 1914 Scott eloped with the dean of Tulane's School of Tropical Medicine to Brazil where they spent six years of poverty and hardship (chronicled in her 1923 autobiography, *Escapade*). On her return to the States, she settled in Greenwich Village, heartily embracing the bohemian life which included Waldo Frank and William Carlos Williams. In 1929, she published the most successful of her nine novels, *The Wave*. She was also a poet and author of four books for children.

Ben Wasson, Faulkner's agent, sent the manuscript of *The Sound and the Fury* to her. Scott's enthusiastic one-page reply ("a novel with the qualities of greatness") was turned into a promotional pamphlet which Cape & Smith issued in advance of the book.

Praising the Benjy section in particular, Scott wrote: "The author is very often able to see here as one of the gods, remote, and at the same time immanent in all the emotions so inevitable to his creatures." And she concluded: "Dilsey is beautiful. Luster is perfect. Mrs. Compson is good. Jason is a devil that, as you are compelled to the vision of the gods, you must compassionate. (Blotner, 627–28).

Caroline Gordon (1895–1981)

Kentucky-born writer and teacher, Gordon and her husband, Allen Tate, met Hemingway in Paris in 1929. A few months later he invited them to a memorable party at Gertrude Stein's apartment, memorable because Fitzgerald was also present and it was the last time Stein, Hemingway, and Fitzgerald were ever together. (See James R. Mellow, *Hemingway: A Life without Consequences*, 393).

The Tates first met Faulkner in October, 1931 at a conference of Southern writers in Charlottesville, Virginia. "Caroline, who admired his work tremendously, deplored his behavior, especially when he spat a drink on a new dress that she had made herself. 'He was trying to say "Yes ma'am," and the drink he had just taken went the wrong way and there was a geyser in which I was engulfed.'" (From a letter to Leonie Adams, cited in Ann Waldron, *Close Connections: Caroline Gordon and the Southern Renaissance*, 105).

Another account of the Charlottesville conference is implied in Stark Young's letter (Nov. 10, 1931) to Ellen Glasgow (who was also in attendance):

I hear that Bill Faulkner was somewhat in absentia in many ways. Not a bad move: it will convince most of the authors that he is all the more a genius, especially those who live in New York. (cited in Pilkington, 372–73).

A recipient in Paris of one of the first copies of *A Farewell to Arms*, Allen Tate told Hemingway

truthfully . . . that he thought it was a masterpiece. Caroline agreed. John Bishop told Allen that the only novelist Hemingway liked was Scott Fitzgerald . . . [and] chose his friends from among the poets. (Waldron, 74).

In a letter to Janice Biala (c.1933), Caroline reports that Gertrude Stein and Alice Toklas were reading Faulkner and

Miss Toklas says she is just too excited over the story of *Sanctuary* which she hears is very interesting. (Waldron, 118).

In a letter to Brainard "Lon" Cheney (c.1937), she urged him to study Flaubert and Hardy,

and it wouldn't do you any harm to study Hemingway for his beautiful sense of form and for his dialogue. (Waldron, 116).

In a newspaper interview (c.1945):

Falsification of detail seems to me the unforgivable sin in a fiction writer. Mr. Faulkner for instance has a livelier imagination than Mr. Erskine Caldwell and swells his characters to monstrous proportions or shrinks them below human level, but he never falsifies sensuous details. I know the insides of his country stores smell just the way he tells me they smell and have the same things on the shelves. (Waldron, 229–30).

Letter to Allen Tate (c.1955):

> You are having a devil of a time about your work but you have
> yet to repeat yourself as Hemingway does, or make an ass of
> yourself, as Faulkner did in his last book. . . . (Waldron, 332–33).

Donald Davidson (1893–1968) and
Allen Tate (1899–1979)

Davidson, a Tennessean, and Tate, a Kentuckian, both of them teachers, poets, and critics along with John Crowe Ransom at Vanderbilt
University, were founding members in the early 1920s of the "Fugitives," a group of southern literary conservatives whose periodical,
The Fugitive, stirred controversy and profoundly influenced the direction of critical thought.

"Tate's approach to the meaning of the South remained symbolic
. . . and relatively detached . . . a cosmopolitan intellectualism. . . .
Davidson's vision is more 'pre-cosmopolitan,' a society that is stable,
religious, more rural than urban, and politically conservative . . .
rooted in family, blood-kinship, clanship, folkways, custom, and
community." (From the foreword by Louis P Simpson, *The Literary
Correspondence of Donald Davidson and Allen Tate*, eds. John T. Fain
and Thomas D. Young, xiii–xiv).

Davidson on Hemingway's *A Farewell to Arms*:

> Ernest Hemingway's characterizations in *A Farewell to Arms*
> were obviously influenced by behaviorism, Davidson noted (in
> "A Critic's Almanac," Nashville *Tennessean*, November 3,
> 1929), and the mere tabulating of the bare facts and the reduction
> of style 'to its lowest and most natural terms' were the result, he

suggested, of an unsuccessful attempt to combine science and art. (Cited by Virginia Rock, "Dualisms in Agrarian Thought," *The Mississippi Quarterly* (Spring, 1960), 88).

Tate's letter to Davidson (Dec. 12, 1929):

You speak of his [Hemingway] writing as 'scientific ministration.' Please, for my sake and for the sake of English prose, look at Hemingway again. I hereby accuse you of taking a thesis to Hemingway and coming away with it proved. There is nothing scientific about Hemingway. And if you think he is a realist, then realism must be redefined. He is unquestionably one of the great stylists of English prose, and it is not his fault if a horde of damn fools have taken him up.... We must not get so lost in our vision of what novelists should do to the Southern scene that we reject the version of "reality" given us by writers who are not Southern.... We cannot afford to admire only those writers who explicitly support our thesis. Now . . . if you look closely enough, Hemingway really supports it: in other words he is a Yankee writer whom we would do well to capture . . . Hemingway's characters come to him through observation . . . the European milieu of mixed Europeans and Americans. Whether or not you like the kind of people he has had to observe, the very fact that he sticks to concrete experience, to a sense of the *pure present*, is of immense significance for us. Hemingway, in fact, has that sense of a stable world, of a total sufficiency of character, which we miss in modern life. He is one of the most irreconcilable reactionaries I have ever met; he hates everything that we hate, although of course he has no historical scene to fall back on . . . if Hemingway were a Southerner he would be just the novelist we are looking for—he would present us without any thesis at all. In other words the ideal Southern novelist is the ideal novelist anywhere—I don't mean that Hemingway is the ideal novelist, only that he is nigh perfect in his own job. . . . (Fain, 244–45).

Davidson's response to Tate (December, 1929):

> I discussed his book (*A Farewell to Arms*) very harshly . . . as a misguided application of science (. . . behavioristic psychology) to literature. . . . I must confess that I extended myself at Hemingway's expense . . . I sacrificed Hemingway . . . in order to make a point against science . . . I felt that he was exposed to criticism, or at least to debate, on this particular point. I certainly respect him, and I'm glad to have your opinion of him to take to heart. . . . (Fain, 248–49).

Erskine Caldwell (1903–87)

Son of an itinerant Presbyterian minister with whom he observed the grim lives of Georgia sharecroppers, Caldwell won immediate fame with *Tobacco Road* (1932), a brutal but often comically realistic story about Jeeter Lester's futile efforts to grow tobacco on the sterile soil of his Georgia farm. Two years later, an adaptation for the Broadway stage by Jack Kirkland opened and ran for more than seven years and over 3,000 performances. Although Caldwell published fifty-five books, only one other novel, *God's Little Acre* (1933), achieved any success.

Caldwell never met Hemingway, but he remembered two meetings with Faulkner—once in Paris at a banquet during the 1930s and once more, in New York, adding, "I was not well acquainted with him," that all they ever discussed was how difficult it was to talk to anyone in a foreign language one didn't know. (Elizabeth Pell Broadwell and Ronald Wesley Hong, interview in *The Georgia Review*, cited in *Conversations with Erskine Caldwell*, ed. Edwin T. Arnold, 198).

Conversation with Richard B. Sale (1970):

> I do read a few books a year, maybe four or five. What has been my habit . . . is to read one book of a writer whom I have heard of as being worth reading . . . I read one book of Faulkner which I liked very much . . . *As I Lay Dying*, which was not a sensational book. It was a solid book. So I formed my opinion of it on just that one instance. . . . One book only. That's all I read. I read one book of Hemingway . . . one book of Sherwood Anderson . . . since that bracket of time, I'm at a loss to pick out anybody I consider in the same field. . . . Because I don't think contemporary fiction is as good as it was. (From a "conversation" with Richard B. Sale, "Studies in the Novel," 3 (Fall, 1971. Cited in *Conversations*, 133).

In response to a question as to whether he thought Faulkner's work offered a "true picture of the South": ". . . I don't think there is a true picture of any region, South or otherwise. It's the interpretation of truth or reality that really makes a work outstanding. . . . Did Faulkner write about life as it is? Sure he did. But it was not a reproduction of life. It was a creation of life, and therefore it was much sharper, much more than the reality of it would have been. I think that any great writer has that same ability." (Conversation with Jac Tharpe. Cited in *Conversations*, 142).

Asked whether he thought that Steinbeck deserved the 1962 Nobel Prize for Literature: "Well, I think he deserved it in a way, but I was surprised that other people were passed over. . . .

"I would certainly say Hemingway because I think he had the ability to produce what other writers could not do. I didn't always like what he wrote. After he began writing novels, I sort of lost interest in Hemingway because I'm an aficionado of short stories. But just for his short stories, I would say he was deserving of any award.

"As for Faulkner, I thought Faulkner was a choice that had to be made worldwide, for the fact that he had a lucidity, an ability to make clear through a very dark screen, make a clarity that you would never get just by a bland looking at people or looking at life. You had to look through this screen." ("Conversation with Jac Tharpe," Cited in *Conversations*, 141).

Cleanth Brooks (1906–94) and Allen Tate (1899–1979)

Tate's letter to Brooks (Jan. 24, 1963):

> . . . Your essay on *Sanctuary* is the best thing on F. I have ever seen: *what happens*, not vague talk about guilt and slavery. . . . (*Cleanth Brooks and Allen Tate: Collected Letters*, ed. Alphonse Vinh, 213).

Tate's letter to Brooks (Jan. 11, 1964):

> Your Faulkner is a very fine book, (*William Faulkner: The Yoknapatawpha Country*) I should never have seen certain things in *Sanctuary* without your guidance. You are the critic, except Red (Robert Penn Warren), who has seen him from the inside. . . .

Tate notes that not all reviewers have agreed, citing especially Marvin Mudrick's observation in the *New York Review of Books* (Jan. 9, 1964) that Brooks had reverted with a rebel whoop to the Confederacy . . .

a Southern blend of vitriol, tart courtliness . . . stultifying trivia and uninhibited hero worship. . . . (Vinh, 213–14).

John Crowe Ransom (1888–1974)

Tennessee–born, a veteran of World War I, and a member of the Vanderbilt faculty in the 1920s, Ransom was, as much as anyone, the leader of the "Fugitives." A distinguished poet and critic, he established the influential writing program at Kenyon College in 1939 and was the founding editor of *The Kenyon Review*.

Letter to Allen Tate (July 17, 1946):

> A big idea has taken hold of us. Next year Faulkner is fifty years old; why not a very fine Faulkner of this (Kenyon) Review? . . . Apparently Faulkner's literature is not engagée enough for New York critics, so that he is in the position of a prophet who will not be honored at home till the visible honors come from abroad. (*Selected Letters of John Crowe Ransom*, eds. Thomas Daniel Young and George Core, 330–331. See below the reference to Clifton Fadiman's review of *Absalom, Absalom!*).

Thomas Wolfe (1900–38)

Maxwell Perkins, Wolfe's editor, argued that no writer was ever less in need of a biographer, so full and candid was the autobiographical content of his fiction. Born in Asheville, North Carolina (which was to become his fictional Altamont), and an overwhelming presence at six and a half feet, Wolfe lived intensely, wrote torrentially, and suffered an untimely and painful death of tubercular lesions which spread from his lungs to his brain. His debut novel, *Look Homeward, Angel: A Story of the Buried Life* (1929), explodes with bursts of lyrical passion and anguish as it follows the journey of its autobiographical hero, Eugene Gant, from childhood in Altamont to young manhood in New York City. Whatever its flaws of rhetorical excess—Wolfe described himself as a "great putter-inner," in the tradition of Balzac, rather than a Flaubertian "taker-outer"—the novel remains an unforgettable portrait of adolescence which has deservedly captured the imagination and affection of young readers for decades. None of his succeeding novels is quite so compelling, although some of his short stories, especially "Only the Dead Know Brooklyn," have sustained interest. As with the related problem in Hart Crane's work, one cannot but speculate whether maturity might have brought to each some mastery of form over the titanic energies that drove them.

In *A Farewell to Arms*,

> [Hemingway] says one thing and suggests two more; his words not only pull their own weight in a sentence, they also pull a very rich weight of profound and moving association and inference. (Unpublished fragment cited in Andrew Turnbull, *Wolfe*, 194).

Letter to Max Perkins (June 21, 1935):

> I have a letter . . . with quoted excerpts—which informs me that *Scribner's* [magazine] carried three *printed* attacks on me—one from Miss Evelyn Scott, one from Mr. Ernest Hemingway—the Big Big He Man and Fighter With Words who can't take it. . . . [see below].

Hemingway had written about Wolfe in *Scribner's* (June, 1935): "I wonder if it would make a writer of him, give him the necessary shock to cut the overflow of words and give him a sense of proportion, if they sent Tom Wolfe to the Dry Tortugas. Maybe it would and maybe it wouldn't. He seemed sad, really, like [Primo] Carnera." (Cited in *The Letters of Thomas Wolfe*, ed. Elizabeth Nowell, 468).

Letter to Stark Young (March 7, 1936):

> . . . I don't think I misunderstood you at all in what you said about Faulkner. . . . And I agree utterly with your estimate in your letter—that what he writes is not like the South, but yet the South is *in* his books, and in the spirit that creates them. (Nowell, *Letters*, 495).

Wolfe is responding here to Young's letter of March 2, 1936: "Underneath a face that looks as mild as one's arse, I am such an excitable fool that I can't always be sure I say what I mean. When you asked a question about my knowing Bill Faulkner, I am not sure I ever made clear what I mean. All I wanted to say was one thing—this—it's ridiculous to imagine Bill a realist depicting the world around him. That world is inside him. His gift is essentially poetic—not to write poetry, necessarily, but to transform and recreate—it is all a sort of Gothicism that he achieves. Not to know this is not to know his quality or his gifts." (*Stark Young: A Life in the Arts, Letters, 1900–1962*, ed. John Pilkington, 671).

Young, almost twenty years older than Faulkner, met him through Phil Stone, an Oxford, Mississippi lawyer, and was sufficiently impressed to invite Faulkner to New York and get him a job in Elizabeth Prall's bookstore. (See also Sherwood Anderson, above.) Young's letter of Nov. 25, 1950 (Pilkington, 1155–56) tries to set the record straight.

Stone, who originally encouraged Faulkner to think of himself as a novelist, noted in 1925 that Faulkner regarded Hemingway at that time as "the greatest American fictionist." (Blotner, 448). And, after reading Young's *So Red the Rose*, Stone told Faulkner (in a remark which is more revealing of Stone's grandiosity than his literary perspicacity): ". . . if I could fuse his mind and yours into one . . . I could make of it a writer of the first class." (Cited in Pilkington, 581n.).

In an interview with May Cameron, the *New York Evening Post*, (May 14, 1936) Wolfe expressed his admiration for Hemingway's work and for Faulkner whose *Sanctuary*, *The Sound and the Fury*, and *As I Lay Dying* he had read. (Cited in Turnbull, *Wolfe*, 341).

THREE

The Poets Sing: On and Off Key

*A*lthough only a few of the poets cited here (as well as those who appeared earlier in "Sounds of the South") were personally acquainted with Hemingway or Faulkner, it is fair to note that both novelists—and especially Hemingway—were prominent figures in the cultural world by the early 1930s and the poets were intensely aware of their radical artistic intentions. It should also be noted that it was as poets that Hemingway and Faulkner first broke into print (Faulkner often characterized himself as "a failed poet") and they maintained a steady professional interest in the poetry of their contemporaries. Consequently, one might infer a rich mutual and influential relationship between their developing fictional mastery and the work of their poetic contemporaries.

T. S. Eliot had already defined as a central fact of the post-World War I decade the dissociation of sensibility, a loss of discipline and authority in modern life. The poets whose comments appear in this section sought in their own work to create through language, structure, and acute observation of self and society new conventions or even convictions that might enable fresh poetic vision. They turned to their peers in fiction to discover how the most imaginative talents confronted like problems. In the work of Hemingway and Faulkner, many of them discovered in prose an expression of a quest much like their own.

Ezra Pound (1885–1972)

Although Pound's excesses—affectations in dress and manner—at first irritated Hemingway's more conventional mid-western tastes, he soon yielded to Pound's enthusiasm, shrewd critical insight, and vast literary background. Most importantly, Pound proved a major influence in getting several of Hemingway's poems published in *Poetry* magazine in Chicago as well as two of his earliest publications in Paris, *Three Stories & Ten Poems* and *in our time*. As with Anderson, Hemingway's personal contact with Pound was relatively brief, a few months each year between 1922 till 1924, but the impact was formidable and the two corresponded for years afterward.

Before he arrived in Paris in 1925 and, as noted, conscientiously avoided meeting others of the so-called Lost Generation, Faulkner had wandered about Italy where he managed—also whether intentioned or not is unknown—to avoid meeting Ezra Pound in Rapallo. He preferred to know the man through his writing. But in 1957, Faulkner joined Hemingway, William Carlos Williams, and others in a successful effort to free Pound from St. Elizabeth's Hospital in Washington, D.C., where he had been confined since 1946 for a combination of treason and insanity. Pound was released in 1958 and returned to Rapallo for his final years.

Letter to William Bird (Rapallo, August 18, 1925):

> Hemingway has been killed by a bull in Saragossa. . . . McAlmon is standing for Parliament . . . good chance of winning. . . . Mr. Ford Madox Ford is personally supervising the erection of a sarcophagus in his honor being erected by the Legion of Honour. . . . Mr. Joyce has gone on a yachting cruise in his son's steam yacht. . . . It is rumored that there are no women among

the party. . . . (*The Letters of Ezra Pound 1907–41*, ed. D. D. Paige, 200).

Letter to James Vogel (Rapallo, January 23, 1929):

. . . Cummings and Hemingway and [Morley] Callaghan are all doing the dollar a word or something of that sort. . . .". (*Letters*, 223).

Ford Madox Ford on Hemingway and Pound:

Mr. Hemingway says that any poet in this century or in the last ten years of the preceding century who can honestly say that he has not been influenced by or learned greatly from the work of Ezra Pound deserves to be pitied rather than rebuked. ("Mediterranean Reverie," *Week-End Review*, 8 (11 Nov. 1933). Cited in Brita Lindberg-Seynsted, ed., *Pound/Ford: The Story of a Literary Friendship*, 132).

Letter to Robert McAlmon (February 2, 1934):

. . . I think you and Hemingway have limited yr. work by not recognizing the economic factor. . . ." (*Letters*, 252).

In a wildly discursive note to Hemingway (Rapallo, November 28, 1936), Pound berates Hemingway too for not addressing economic issues (as he thought Benito Mussolini was), goes on to applaud Hemingway's defense of the working man (Hemingway was writing *To Have and Have Not*) and, in a thoroughly vulgar opera buffa conclusion, Pound mocks Hemingway's shooting innocent lions in Africa instead of greedy bankers at the Bourse in Paris.

T(homas) S(tearns) Eliot (1888–1965)

From the time that Pound lent him a copy of *The Waste Land* in 1923, Hemingway was intimately aware of Eliot's work, committing much of it to memory and often parodying it in his letters. For whatever reason, however, possibly because of what he regarded as Eliot's pompous and effete appearance, Hemingway was never able to resist the temptation to mock the poet, regularly referring to him as "Major" or "Reverend." It is generally assumed that the eponymous protagonists of his short story, "Mr. And Mrs. Elliot" (1924) are aimed at the poet, and he goes out of his way in *Death in the Afternoon* to ridicule him. On the other hand, he commended and supported Eliot in the latter's effort to have Pound released from St. Elizabeth's.

On the commemoration of Thomas Hardy's death, Hemingway wrote:

> If I knew that by grinding Mr. Eliot into a fine dry powder and sprinkling that powder over Mr. Conrad's grave Mr. Conrad would shortly appear. . . . I would leave for London tomorrow morning with a sausage grinder. . . . you cannot couple T. S. Eliot and Joseph Conrad in a sentence seriously . . . and not laugh. (*transatlantic*, 2,3 (September, 1924), 341–2).

In spite of Hemingway's abuse, Eliot consistently voiced admiration for Hemingway:

> Mr. Hemingway is a writer for whom I have considerable respect; he seems to me to tell the truth about his own feelings at the moment when they exist. ("Commentary," *The Criterion* [April, 1933], 471).

> I have been waiting for another book by Mr. Scott Fitzgerald with more eagerness and curiosity than I should feel toward the

work of any of his contemporaries except that of Mr. Ernest Hemingway. Eliot's blurb for *Tender Is the Night* (1933). (Cited in Scott Donaldson, *Hemingway and Fitzgerald: The Rise and Fall of a Literary Friendship*, 171).

Letter from Hemingway to Harvey Breit, July 9, 1950:

Well I guess, some of us write and some of us pitch but so far there isn't any law a man has to go and see the Cocktail Party by T. S. Eliot from St. Louis where Yogi Berra comes from. 'Royalist, Anglo-Catholic and conservative.' A damned good poet and a fair critic; but he can kiss my ass as a man and he never hit the ball out of the infield in his life and he would not have existed except for dear old Ezra, the lovely poet and stupid traitor. (Baker, *Selected Letters*, 701).

Eliot's poetry, especially "The Love Song of J. Alfred Prufrock" and *The Waste Land*, were deep influences on Faulkner, first, and almost slavishly, in his own poetry, and later in his fiction—as in the Prufrockian character of Horace Benbow in *Sanctuary*.

William Carlos Williams (1883–1963)

Although it is generally recognized that Gertrude Stein was godmother to Hemingway's first son, John (nicknamed Bumby), the equally interesting fact that Williams performed the circumcision is often overlooked. (See Paul Mariani, *William Carlos Williams: A New World Naked*, 239; Michael Reynolds, *Hemingway: The Paris Years*, 209).

Letter to Louis Zukofsky, (December 22, 1929):

And here was Hemingway becoming 'the modern Playboy of the Western World,' even though—like Pound—he [Williams] was convinced that McAlmon was finally the better writer. (Mariani, 294).

A recurrent sub-theme in Mariani's biography finds Williams constantly comparing his friend McAlmon to Hemingway and wondering about the mysteries of failure and success in art. In this he may have been influenced by Pound's opinions. Katherine Anne Porter seems to have felt a similar preference for McAlmon.

Letter to John Herrmann (October 25, 1931) when Williams was editing *Contact*:

> I don't want just raw stuff . . . but I do want a contact without literary *side* Hemingway's first stories . . . had had the feel for the kind of thing he was looking for. But that was before Hemingway had gone in for "telling arrangement" and "feeling." (Mariani, 321).

Marianne Moore (1887–1972)

The doyenne of American women poets was born in St. Louis but became a long-term resident of Brooklyn, the influential editor of *The Dial* (1925–29) and a fan of the Brooklyn Dodgers, beloved for her black cape and tricornered hat. Her first volume, *Poems* (1921), was published in England without her knowledge by her friends, H.D. and Robert McAlmon. Succeeding volumes display precisely wrought and cadenced images which anchor the extraordinary range of her subject matter (bearing out her belief that "poets should present imaginary gardens with real toads in them").

Hemingway in Paris, ca. 1925.

Faulkner in the Luxembourg
Gardens, Paris, 1925.

Sinclair Lewis, ca. 1916.

Edmund Wilson, ca. 1921.   John Peale Bishop, ca.1921.

Sherwood Anderson, ca. 1926.

F. Scott Fitzgerald, soon after his marriage to Zelda, 1921.

Gertrude Stein, Alice B. Toklas, and Carl Van Vechten on an American lecture tour, 1934.

Harry Crosby and Kay Boyle at The Mill, Crosby's estate near Paris, 1929.

Hemingway at Schruns, Austria, with John Dos Passos (r.) and Gerald Murphy, 1925–26.

T. S. Eliot, ca. 1954.

Archibald MacLeish, Librarian of Congress, ca. 1941.

Dawn Powell, 1940.   Eudora Welty, n.d.

Glenway Wescott (l.), Malcolm Cowley, and Allen Tate (r.) at their election to the American Academy of Arts and Letters, 1964.

Hemingway at his home, Finca Vigia, Havana, Cuba, receiving the Nobel Prize from the Swedish Minister, 1954.

Faulkner at Stockholm, Sweden, with Bertrand Russell, both receiving the Nobel Prize, December 1949.

Hemingway in the gun room at his home in Ketchum, Idaho, 1960.

Faulkner at home in Oxford, Mississippi, 1960.

Letter to Ezra Pound (July 29, 1932):

> [I] am growing hard toward callers of the kind that ask you as
> you are being carried on a stretcher from your house to an am-
> bulance, which you think is the greatest—William Faulkner,
> Robinson Jeffers, or Josephine Baker. (*Selected Letters of Mari-
> anne Moore*, ed. Bonnie Costello, 275).

Letter to John Warner Moore (December 18, 1932):

> . . . I told the S.P.C.A. they might ask Prof. W. L. Phelps . . . to
> protest; that his opinion has great weight and that he had spoken
> against Ernest Hemingway's Death in the Afternoon. . . ."

Moore felt that a Universal Pictures proposed film version of the
book might have unfortunate consequences, helping to "prepare sentiment on the part of people for bull-fights in America unless Hemingway has delivered an estocado to the gizzard beforehand."
(*Letters*, 285).

Louise Bogan (1897–1970)

Closely linked to her mentor, Edmund Wilson, and later an intimate
friend of Theodore Roethke, Bogan was admired for both her poetry
(its language and imagery evocative of the Elizabethan-Metaphysical
tradition) and her critical eye. She was poetry editor of *The New
Yorker* for almost four decades.

Letter to Ruth Benedict (April 9, 1926):

> I've discovered a wonderful man—Ernest Hemingway—who
> can really write simple declarative sentences. He has a book

called *In Our Time*, published by Boni and Liveright, that's thrilling. (*What the Woman Lived: Selected Letters of Louise Bogan*, ed. Ruth Limmer, 27).

Letter to Morton D. Zabel (August 22, 1937):

> I saw The Spanish Earth this afternoon. . . . Hemingway was just too noble and humanitarian, and clipped-speech throughout. You'd have thought that he'd never whooped up such a humanitarian spectacle as a bull-fight in his life, or never been passed bottles of beer by minions while on safari. All full of the milk of human kindness, and the virtues of the dear peasants and the brave civilians. I don't see him doing any labor and union helping at home, however. I suppose an automobile strike isn't colorful enough for him. (*Selected Letters*, 162).

Much less publicly than Hemingway, in a response to an appeal by the League of American Writers, Faulkner signed a statement in 1938 opposing "Franco and fascism . . . and outrages against the people of Republican Spain." He backed up his antifascist stance by sending his first-draft manuscript of *Absalom, Absalom!* to Vincent Sheean as a contribution to a relief fund for the Spanish Loyalists. (Blotner, 1030).

Hart Crane (1899–1932)

Alcoholic, homosexual, preternaturally gifted, Crane stormed recklessly between New York, France, and the Caribbean. Despite his inner torments, Crane had already established himself as one of America's great visionary poets, rejecting the pessimism of Eliot's "wasteland," and using the same Brooklyn Bridge that inspired Whitman for his own flawed but majestic masterwork, *The Bridge*. After a year in Mexico (where Katherine Anne Porter let him live at her house until his alcoholic binges became intolerable), Crane jumped to his death into "that great wink of eternity" from the stern of the ship that was returning him to New York.

Letter to Susan Jenkins and William Slater Brown (February 16, 1927):

> . . . I've been reading The Cock also Rises . . . and have developed a perfect case of acidosis. No wonder the book sold; there isn't a sentence in it without a highball or a martini in it to satisfy the suppressed desires of the public. It's a brilliant and a terrible book. The fiesta and the bullfight best. No warmth, no charm in it whatever, but of course Hemingway doesn't want such. (*O My Land, My Friends: The Selected Letters of Hart Crane*, eds. Langdon Hammer and Brom Weber, 318).

Letter to Yvor Winters (January 27, 1928):

> *Men without Women* is a book you ought to read. The short story called "The Killers" makes one doff one's hat. (*Letters*, 359).

Carl Sandburg (1878–1967)

Hemingway and Sandburg met in 1921 at Kenley Smith's apartment in Chicago where Sandburg read from poems recently published in *Poetry*. Hemingway's admiration for Sandburg never lapsed and after winning the Nobel Prize, Hemingway told Harvey Breit in a telephone conversation (October 28, 1954): "I would have been happy

. . . today if the prize had gone to the beautiful writer Isak Dinesen, to Bernard Berenson . . . and I would have been most happy to know that the prize had been awarded to Carl Sandburg. . . . " He later explained that "it was not too small a thing to have made three people happy . . . especially since all of them were elderly." (Baker, *Hemingway*, 527–28).

Faulkner would have disagreed (see Conrad Aiken above), despising what he decried as Sandburg's "sentimental Chicago propaganda." ("Books & Things," *The Mississippian*, Feb. 16, 1921; reprinted in *William Faulkner: Early Prose and Poetry*, ed. Carvel Collins, 75).

Letter to S. A. Marshall (January 23, 1962):

> Something like thirty-two years ago I was joined with Hemingway in our affection for the Desplains River which ran between his hometown Oak Park and my hometown Maywood. Far later he was the first and only recipient of the Nobel prize [*sic*] to say to the Associated Press that if the decision had been with him he would have named me. (*The Letters of Carl Sandburg*, ed. Herbert Mitgang.)

Wallace Stevens (1879–1955)

In one of the more unlikely and bizarre literary confrontations, The Man with the Blue Guitar met The Battler in late February, 1936. As is inevitable in such cases, strict reportage is impossible, but the general details are relatively clear. In Key West on his annual vacation, the ("well-lit") fifty-seven-year-old Vice-President of Hartford Accident and Indemnity Company seems to have bad-mouthed Hemingway in the presence of Hemingway's sister, Ursula, who was visiting her brother at the time. Ernest, also "well-lit," stormed out of his house to protect the family honor and fortuitously encountered Stevens on the street, where blows were exchanged. Hemingway seems to have scored one (possibly two) knockdowns and Stevens managed a shot at the Hemingway jaw. Apologizing to Ursula and Ernest on the following day, and bearing a bruised eye and broken hand, Stevens asked Hemingway to keep quiet about the incident, fearing recriminations in Hartford. Each combatant, being a man of words rather than a man of his word, immediately broke the compact, Stevens telling the story to his Key West friends a few days later (Peter Brazeau, *Parts of a World: Wallace Stevens Remembered*, 98). See also Hemingway's gleeful account written to Sara Murphy and Dos Passos (Carlos Baker, ed. *Selected Letters*, 438, 446). By 1951, the incident seems to have become a cherished anecdote for Stevens with himself as hero, as he was delighted to recount to E. E. Cummings and Monroe Wheeler (Brazeau, 191). Most remarkably, Stevens did not let his personal distaste for Hemingway color his admiration for his achievements and he was especially gratified to be informed by his young Cuban friend, Rodriguez Feo, that Hemingway "thought Wallace Stevens a great poet." (Richardson, *Wallace Stevens*, 244).

For further details, see among other accounts, the following: Baker, *Hemingway*, 345; Reynolds, *Hemingway: The 1930s*, 221–22; Richardson, *Wallace Stevens*, 124–125; See also Louise Bogan's letter to Morton Zabel (December 12, 1935) in *What the Woman Lived: Selected Letters of Louise Bogan, 1920–1970*, Ed., Ruth Limmer, 12. Bogan's information derives from Edmund Wilson to whom Dos Passos forwarded the story. Bogan's letter seems to be misdated.

In 1954, Faulkner and Stevens shared the dais at the National Book Award where each was to be honored—Stevens for poetry, Faulkner for fiction. Faulkner was introduced by Clifton Fadiman—but was apparently unaware of or indifferent to this man who had written a devastating (and wrong-headed) review of *Absalom, Absalom!* (1936). Faulkner read a brief speech, inaudibly, and quickly left the room. (See Blotner, *Faulkner*, 2, 1524–1525; Karl, *Faulkner*, 901).

It is worth noting that the "New York critics" were slow to bestow much respect on Faulkner's work. See Clifton Fadiman's notorious *New Yorker* review of *Absalom, Absalom!*: "The most consistently boring novel by a reputable writer to come my way during the past decade" (October 31, 1936). And although Granville Hicks had praised Faulkner's technical skill in September, 1931 (Bookman, 84:1), in *The Great Tradition* (1939), he described his work as "dangerously close to triviality."

This possible New York animus seems to have had amazing endurance, as manifest in a *New York Times* editorial commenting on Faulkner's selection as a Nobel Laureate: "His field of vision is concentrated on a society that is too often vicious, depraved, decadent, corrupt. Americans must fervently hope that the award . . . does not mean that foreigners admire him because he gives them a picture of American life they believe to be typical and true . . . Incest and rape may be common pastimes in Faulkner's 'Jefferson, Miss.' but they are not elsewhere in the United States." (Nov. 11, 1950) (Cited In Millgate, *Achievement*, 48).

———————

Letter to Henry Church (July 2,1942):

   . . . Your subject, when you come to think of it, is a terrifying subject: ACTUALITY. . . . Given an actuality extraordinary enough, it has a vitality all its own which makes it independent of any conjunction with the imagination. The perception of the

POETRY OF EXTRAORDINARY ACTUALITY is . . . a job for a man capable of going his own way. . . .

What I am trying to lead up to is the idea that the anti-poet may be the right man to discuss EXTRAORDINARY ACTUALITY and by discussing it in his own way reveal the poetry of the thing. . . .

Now, the best man I can think of for the job is Ernest Hemingway . . . Most people don't think of Hemingway as a poet, but obviously he is a poet and I should say, offhand, the most significant of living poets, so far as the subject of EXTRAORDINARY ACTUALITY is concerned. . . .

But supposing that Hemingway shouldn't be available: What about Faulkner? He is my second suggestion. For all his gross realism, Faulkner is a poet. (*Letters of Wallace Stevens*, ed. Holly Stevens, 411–12).

Robert Frost (1874–1963)

". . . when he learned of the death by suicide of Ernest Hemingway. For some time afterward, he could talk and think of nothing else, and he felt sure that he knew just why Hemingway had done what he had done: he had become convinced that he had lost his ability to write. Frost would not tolerate any criticism of Hemingway's action. He insisted that he had shown great courage in killing himself when the thing he had lived for was gone. . . ." (Lawrance Thompson and R. H. Winnick, *Robert Frost: The Later Years*, 294).

Among the memorials in the *New York Times* (July 3, 1961), Frost wrote: "Ernest Hemingway was rough and unsparing with life. He was rough and unsparing with himself . . . Fortunately for us, if it is a time to speak of fortune, he gave himself time to make his greatness.

His style dominated our story-telling long and short. I remember the fascination that made me want to read aloud "The Killers" to everybody that came along. He was a friend I shall miss. The country is in mourning."

At a Writers' Conference in Boulder, Colorado (July, 1935) in which Robert Penn Warren delivered a talk on "The Recent Southern Novel," he (Frost) told John Bartlett that he loathed all "the writings of Faulkner—he had never been able to read through a single one of them." (Lawrance Thompson, *Robert Frost: The Years of Triumph*, 424).

Lawrance Thompson reports that Frost told him that he felt Faulkner's Nobel Prize Acceptance Speech with its belief that mankind would not only "endure" but "prevail" was "insincere and full of cant." (Thompson and Winnick, 422, n.6)

While in his twenties, Faulkner admitted joining "the pack belling loudly after contemporary poets. I could not always tell what it was about but 'This is the stuff,' I told myself. . . ." ("Verse Old and Nascent: A Pilgrimage," *Double Dealer*, 7 (April, 1925), adding, "That page is closed to me forever. I read Robinson and Frost with pleasure, and Aldington; Conrad Aiken's minor music still echoes in my heart . . . I no longer try to read the others at all. . . ." After alluding to his pleasure with Housman, Shakespeare, Spenser, Keats, and Shelley, Faulkner concludes, "Is there not among us someone who can write something beautiful and passionate and sad instead of saddening?" (Collins, Carvel, ed., *William Faulkner: Early Prose and Poetry*, 116–118).

Hilda Doolittle [H.D.] (1886–1961)

As a student at Bryn Mawr, Doolittle formed a lifelong friendship with William Carlos Williams, met Marianne Moore, and became temporarily affianced to Ezra Pound. In 1911, she embarked for London, where Pound had launched the Imagist school of poetry. She soon became one of the leaders of the Imagists, her work appearing frequently in Harriet Monroe's *Poetry*. Despite her physical fragility, she worked and loved vigorously. Novelist as well as poet, she also translated from the Greek, and, while her husband, the poet and novelist Richard Aldington was away during World War I, she edited his literary magazine, *Egoist*. After their marriage failed, she enjoyed a liaison with D. H.Lawrence (perhaps bearing his child), and settled at last as permanent consort to Bryher (Winifred Ellerman), the lesbian British novelist married (for convenience) to the bisexual Robert McAlmon (see McAlmon, p. 52).

After reading Faulkner's *Pylon* and comparing American with British prose (c. 1937), she "admired Faulkner's move from a Jamesian dominance into '. . . skyrockets of prose that without James would probably remain inchoate, but with that as Background are consummate Art. One thinks and wonders at the language itself. How Americans do put drive and push and punch into it. . . .'" (Barbara Guest, *Herself Defined: The Poet H.D. and Her World*, 236).

In conversation with Lionel Durand (April, 1960), she confessed that "she had become, from her recent reading, fonder of Faulkner and Hemingway" (Guest, 320).

E. E. Cummings (1894–1962)

Letter to Ezra Pound (April 14, 1935) referring to Arnold Gingrich's comparative payments for contributions to *Esquire*:

Re thy financial queery: Oinis is paid $450, on dit, for his monthly crap . . . pretty damn shitty. . . . [Cummings had been paid $150]. (*Selected Letters of E. E. Cummings*, eds. F. W. Dupee and George Stade, 142).

———

At least from the time of his marriage to Pauline Pfeiffer and the publication of *A Farewell to Arms*, Hemingway's financial situation was sufficient to support a lifestyle which included extensive travel, safaris, deep-sea fishing, and more than comfortable housing. Along with the royalties from his novels, he received top dollar for his stories and reportage, and he negotiated shrewdly with Hollywood, securing the highest price ever yet paid for film rights for a book (*For Whom the Bell Tolls* to Paramount Pictures for $136,000 in October, 1940).

Faulkner, on the other hand, spent most of the 1930s and the War years scrabbling desperately to meet monthly bills in spite of what were, for the times, very decent Hollywood contracts. In a letter to Robert Haas of Random House in May, 1940, he vents his feelings in true Faulknerian fashion: "Every so often . . . I take these fits of sort of raging and impotent exasperation at this . . . paradox which my life reveals. Beginning at the age of thirty I, an artist . . . began to become the sole, principal and partial support—food, shelter, heat, clothes, medicine, kotex, school fees, toilet paper and picture shows—of my mother . . . [a] brother's widow and child, a wife of my own and two step children, my own child; I inherited my father's debts and his dependents, white and black without inheriting yet from anyone one inch of land or one stick of furniture . . . I bought without help from anyone the house I live in and all the furniture; I bought my farm the same way. I am 42 years old and I have already paid for four funerals and will certainly pay for one more and in all likelihood two more beside that . . . before I ever come to my own." (Blotner, *Letters*, 122–123).

Theodore Roethke (1908–63)

Letter to Hemingway (July 13, 1953). "It's my belief that you prose writers should look at the versifiers once in a while. . . . I grew up in Michigan and have fished your country there; often have hoped to meet you in the flesh and to exchange views on such subjects as What Greb-or-any-smart-hooker-could do to Marciano, etc." Accompanying the letter was the poem "Song for the Squeeze Box," about which Roethke noted, "I thought enclosed doggerel in which you are mentioned might amuse you." (from Allan Seager's *The Glass House: The Life of Theodore Roethke*, 196).

> From "SONG FOR THE SQUEEZE BOX"
>
> It wasn't Ernest; it wasn't Scott—
> The boys I knew when I went to pot;
> They didn't boast; they didn't snivel,
> But stepped right up and swung at the Devil;
> After exchanging a punch or two,
> They all sat down like me and you
> —And began to drink up the money.

Elizabeth Bishop (1911–79)

Her output was spare—fewer than a hundred in her *Complete Poems* (1969 National Book Award)—but readers have pored ceaselessly and admiringly over her deeply felt, painterly descriptions of place, works which brought her numerous awards, including the Pulitzer (1955). "I think geography comes first in my work," she once said. "And then animals. But I like people too. I've written a few poems about people."

A lesbian (her long-time Brazilian lover, Lota de Macedo Soares, committed suicide), she enjoyed close friendships with Marianne

Moore and Robert Lowell with whom—among others—she had a rich correspondence.

————————

Letter to Pearl Kazin (December 10, 1952):

I read *The Old Man and the Sea* and like most of it—all except about six of his really horrible lapses—enormously. Such a wonderful sense of the sea and space, etc. (*One Art: Letters Selected and Edited*, ed. Robert Giroux, 252).

Letter to Anne Stevenson (January 8, 1964):

I admire both Hemingway and Lawrence—along with others—for living in the real world and knowing how to do things. (*The Elizabeth Bishop Papers*, Washington University in St. Louis).

FOUR

Other Voices

The 1930s

*T*hese were the years of the Great Depression, a decade during which spirits as well as economies sagged and the United States, along with the rest of the world, staggered toward the terrible encounter between fascism and democracy. But in the American world of letters, the scene was, if not altogether admirable, certainly animated. The most popular novel of the decade was Margaret Mitchell's *Gone with the Wind* (1936) and, arguably, the most beloved figure, Mickey Mouse. More ambitious literary achievement was also being acknowledged, Sinclair Lewis winning the Nobel Prize in 1930 for *Babbitt* and Robert Frost twice receiving Pulitzer Prizes for his poetry. Others too were publishing significant work: Katherine Anne Porter the superb stories collected in *Flowering Judas* (1930); Fitzgerald his *Tender Is the Night* (1934); Thomas Wolfe's *Of Time and the River* (1935), his sequel to *Look Homeward, Angel* (1929); Dos Passos's *USA* trilogy (1936); Richard Wright, the powerful novellas of *Uncle Tom's Children* (1938); Nathanael West's *The Day of the Locust*, and Steinbeck's *The Grapes of Wrath* in 1939.

Hemingway and Faulkner were also creative during the 1930s—but in significantly different ways. Hemingway began with a masterful blend of tauromachy and literary criticism in *Death in the Afternoon* (1932) and ended the decade with his *Forty Nine Stories* (1938)—which included two of his most accomplished shorter efforts—"The Snows of Kilimanjaro" and "The Short Happy Life of Francis Macomber." Beyond these works, apart from vigorous reporting during the Spanish Civil War, the quality of his writing wilted in the weary prose of *Green Hills of Africa* (1935) and the posturing of *To Have and Have Not* (1937). These were the years when it seemed that Hemingway's creativity was more focused on shaping his image as "Papa," the sportsman/adventurer, than in intensifying his commitment to his craft.

On the other hand, although Faulkner had attained a small notoriety as a Gothic sensationalist with the controversial *Sanctuary* (1931), more quietly and almost below the radar of popular response, he was shaping the finest fiction of his career, among them his masterworks, *As I Lay Dying* (1930), *Light in August* (1932), and *Absalom, Absalom!* (1936).

By the end of the decade, each had a comfortable sense of ascendant accomplishment, Hemingway the euphoric satisfaction of completing his intended epic novel, *For Whom the Bell Tolls,* Faulkner surveying from the heights the literary plain below. Having found Walter Van Tilburg Clark's *Ox-bow Incident* dull, he wrote to Bennett Cerf at Random House: "What has happened to writing anyway? Hemingway and Dos Passos and I are veterans now; we should be fighting tooth and nail to hold our places against younger writers. But there are no young writers worth a damn that I know of. I think of my day. There were Lewis and Dreiser and Sherwood Anderson and so forth, and we were crowding the hell out of them. But now there doesn't seem to be enough pressure behind us to keep Dos Passos and Hemingway writing even. What's your explanation for it?" (*Letters,* July 24, 1940, 134).

To read the comments of their contemporary writers during this troubled decade deepens a sense of how seriously Hemingway and Faulkner were watched—and, on occasion, with how much exasperation.

Theodore Dreiser (1871–1945)

Letter to Vernon C. Sherwin (February 16, 1933):

On the rising generation of writers in the South. The appearance
of such things as 'Souvenir' (a story of a lynching by Sherwin),
Heyward's *Porgy*, *In Abraham's Bosom* . . . Faulkner's *Sanctuary* . . . all these make me feel that the old traditions of the South
are about to die and be replaced by . . . sanity. . . . (*Letters of
Theodore Dreiser*, Volume Two, ed. Robert H. Elias, 624).

H. L. Mencken (1880–1956)

After receiving an inscribed copy of *Men Without Women* from Fitzgerald, Mencken paired Hemingway with Thornton Wilder in his
subsequent review (*American Mercury*, May, 1928):

It is technical virtuosity that has won them attention; it is hard
work and fundamental thinking that must get them on, if they
are to make good their high promise. (Cited in Bruccoli, *Scott
and Ernest: The Fitzgerald-Hemingway Friendship*, 58).

Letter to Dorothy Tillett (January 4, 1935):

. . . I suggest that you give an eye to the dialogue of Hemingway,
especially in the short stories. He is, in many respects, a quack
but he has a sharp ear and reports the vernacular accurately. (*The
New Mencken Letters*, ed. Carl Bode, 339).

Letter to Henry Miller (June 8, 1939): [On *Tropic of Capricorn*]

You achieve with ease all of the effects that Joyce tries to get by
puffing and fluttering and you make such performers as Hemingway look merely silly. (Bode, 443).

Letter to Edgar Kemler (November 1, 1946):

> I had little if anything to do with the early promotion of Scott
> Fitzgerald. When he first appeared he interested me very much,
> but I was convinced that he . . . needed the discipline of hard
> work. . . . In his personal life Scott was a very foolish fellow. His
> belief that Hemingway was a great genius always struck me as
> somewhat ridiculous. When he fell for Gertrude Stein, it was
> plainly half-idiotic. (Bode, 565).

Letter to Georg Katzke (August 13, 1948):

> I recall reading Faulkner's *Sanctuary* some years ago but I have
> forgotten it completely. He wrote some excellent short stories in
> his early days but his novels have always seemed to me to be
> rather forced melodramas. (Bode, 597).

Wyndham Lewis (1882–1957)

A Canadian who settled in England, Wyndham Lewis is the sole non-
American representative among the Hemingway-Faulkner contemporaries in this book. He appears here in part because his diverse if ec-
centric genius gained him fame as an artist (founder of Vorticism),
novelist (*The Apes of God*), and critic (founded and co-edited with
Ezra Pound, *Blast*, a magazine that savaged the literary establishment,
particularly Virginia Woolf and the Bloomsbury Group). More importantly, he needs to be heard as the most singular among the English voices responding to Hemingway and Faulkner during the 1920s
and 1930s. Hemingway's work had already caused a small stir in England, partly due to Pound's promotion and the close connection of
the little magazines between London and Paris. Two or three years

later, Richard Hughes (*A High Wind in Jamaica*) and, surprisingly, the resolutely realistic novelist, Arnold Bennett, had encouraged the British publication of *The Sound and the Fury* and *As I Lay Dying*.

In several essays (collected in *Men Without Art*, 1934) Lewis, who was nothing if not a fierce contrarian, took brutal aim: the first, "The 'Dumb Ox'" is about Hemingway; its companion piece, on Faulkner, bears the title "The Moralist with the Corncob." Lewis mocks "the *steining* of Hemingway" ("this brilliant Jewish lady has made a clown of him by teaching [him] her baby-talk"(26). All that separates him from Gertrude Stein is subject matter; he writes "about prize fighting, war, or the bull ring" (24). Hemingway's voice, Lewis suggests, is the voice of the masses, the slaughterhouse cattle—the "expression of the soul of the dumb-ox," uttered with "bovine genius" (36).

While browsing in Sylvia Beach's bookstore, Hemingway read the article. His outraged reaction was to smash a vase of tulips that Beach had been given for her birthday. (See Noel Riley Fitch, *Sylvia Beach and the Lost Generation: A History of Literary Paris in the Twenties & Thirties*, 343). Hemingway's final response several years after Lewis's death was to describe him as having, beneath his bohemian, wide-brimmed black hat, the eyes of an "unsuccessful rapist." (*A Moveable Feast*, 109).

Lewis writes somewhat less nastily that Faulkner, "is as full of 'passion'—of sound and fury—as Hemingway is austerely without it. He is as hot and sticky as Hemingway is dry and without undue heat." (42). But the lush, the florid, and the poetic elements are too often "pumped in" (too often with unintended comic effect) to create atmosphere when plot and character falter. Although his style lacks the tensile strength of Hemingway's, Faulkner's Yoknapatawpha is, Lewis allows, an unforgettable Creation: ". . . if each and all of his stories is 'a tale told by an idiot'—that doesn't make his Sartorises,

Popeyes, Christmases . . . or Temple Drake, any the less impressive
company, in their hysterical way. All are demented: his novels are,
strictly speaking, clinics." (42).

Sinclair Lewis (1885–1951)

While still a reporter in Toronto, Hemingway began taunting Sinclair
Lewis for both his physical and literary ungainliness. At first, Lewis
tried courteous and admiring responses, but at last joined Hemingway
in ceaseless exchanges of nastiness, culminating eventually in the cruel
caricature of Lewis that Hemingway drew in *Across the River and
Into the Trees*.

There, in a scene at the Gritti Palace Hotel in Venice, Hemingway's
Colonel Cantwell describes a "pitted compatriot, chawing at his food
. . . who speaks bad Italian assiduously . . . and has no taste in either
food or wine. . . . He writes every night . . . even if he has outlived his
talents." (*Across the River and Into the Trees*, 119,124).

Lewis was always generous in his praise of Faulkner (see below),
but in 1949, when Faulkner was about to win his own Nobel Prize,
he wrote to a friend that he would "rather to be in the same pigeon
hole with Dreiser and Sherwood Anderson, than with Sinclair Lewis
and Mrs. Chinahand Buck." (Blotner, *Letters*, 299).

Lewis on hearing of his Nobel Laureate selection (Dec. 1930):

> I should be just as glad if Eugene O'Neill had received it. . . . I'd
> have felt the same way about Ernest Hemingway. He'll get it
> some day, but I suppose he hasn't written enough yet. I think
> Hemingway will get the award in ten years. (Schorer, *Sinclair
> Lewis: An American Life*, 550).

Lewis's Nobel Acceptance Speech (1930) named several young Americans whose writing he admired: Ernest Hemingway, Thomas Wolfe, Wilder, Dos Passos, Stephen Benet, Michael Gold, and, in closing, Faulkner, "who has freed the South from hoopskirts." (Blotner, *Faulkner*, 679).

Centennial issue of *Yale Literary Magazine*, Feb., 1936 (on *Green Hills of Africa*):

> Mister Ernest Hemingway
> Halts his slaughter of the kudu
> To remind you that you may
> Risk his sacerdotal hoodoo
> If you go on, day by day,
> Talking priggishly as you do.
> Speak up, man! Be bravely heard
> Bawling the four-letter word!
> And wear yr mind décolleté
> Like Mr. Ernest Hemingway.
> (cited in Schorer, 616–17).

On *The Sun Also Rises*:

This was the first of the three great novels which have—along with his minor yet still magnificent work—revealed Hemingway as one of the few truly important and almost savagely individual authors living.

On Hemingway's receiving a gold medal for *For Whom the Bell Tolls*: Hemingway was "a lone scarred tree, for the lightning of living has hit him." (Schorer, 680).

Katherine Anne Porter (1890–1980)

There was apparently one awkward meeting in 1934 as Porter chatted with Sylvia Beach at Shakespeare and Company. When Hemingway arrived unexpectedly, Beach grasped each of them by the hand, declaring: "I want the two best modern American writers to know each other." Like negatively charged particles and equally taken aback, both stared at one another speechless for about ten seconds and Hemingway ran out the door. (See Noel Riley Fitch, *Sylvia Beach and the Lost Generation*, 344).

Letter to Caroline Gordon, April 24, 1931:

> At last I got hold of Faulkner's *The Sound and the Fury* and it curdled the marrow in my bones. I have never seen such a cold-blooded assault on the nerve-ends, so unrepentant a statement of horror as that book. And such good bold sound writing. It left me so shaken and unnerved I could hardly believe the face of the sun. . . . But my God! There should be something in a work of art that gives you something to hang onto after the very worst has been told. Still, I want to read *As I Lay Dying. (Letters of Katherine Anne Porter*, ed. Isabel Bayley, 39).

Letter to Monroe Wheeler, December 18, 1946 (referring to French responses to her translated fiction):

> The few reviews I have seen from Paris are really remarkable. They just broke down and took me in and said I was good and that everybody should read me: and invariably they took a smack at Hemingway, Steinbeck, Faulkner, and who is that other one? Saroyan? Caldwell? Both, I think, and the only thing that bothers me is that they mention them all in one breath, not really being able to pick out Hemingway and Faulkner from the others. . . . (Bayley, 329–30).

Letter to Paul Porter, November 11, 1952 (on the reviews of her essay collection, *The Days Before*):

. . . I have had the most unbelievably good reviews, more constantly friendly I daresay than any other writer in this country.
And I suppose my books are the least-sold of any serious writer
here. Look at Hemingway. The reviewers and the critics have
needled him steadily for twenty years, and the worst thing he
writes becomes a best seller overnight. If the newspapers could
kill, he would be dead years ago. (Bayley, 438).

Letter to Seymour Lawrence, April 14, 1957:

. . . I don't mean that Hemingway isn't admirable, and he has
done things his own way that no one else could do at all. I have
watched for years in distress the struggles of that centerless,
mindless, uncreated man to present an image of himself to the
world that will hide, perhaps even from himself, the cureless fear
and the despair that comes of fear—fear of his own human in-
stinct, of his own thoughts, of the feelings of others, of language
itself. . . . (Bayley, 538).

Letter to Jordon Pecile, July 3, 1961 (on Hemingway's suicide):

Well, it's done and finished and this man, such a bore of a man
really and such an incomplete artist, and so pitiable and ill-con-
ducted—I can hardly think of another man of his world fame
who to me was so completely uninteresting and insignificant—
has quite literally taken a whole era into the past with him. He
really represented a period and a place and a point of view, and
he did great harm in the sense that he confirmed mean little
minds and limited intelligences in a kind of Hollywood notion
of the deadpan hero. . . . It's a shock just the same—a very pathetic end, and to think of such despair and such loneliness!
(Bayley, 588).

Henry Miller (1891–1980)

From Brooklyn to Paris to Big Sur, Miller broadcast his Whitman-inspired Romanticism—autobiographical fiction thickly layered with expatriate rebelliousness, innate narcissism, esthetic surrealism, and vivid as well as comic pornography. His best writing (*Tropic of Cancer, Tropic of Capricorn*) was done in Paris during the 1920s but banned in the United States until the 1960s. Among his ardent admirers were T. S. Eliot, Ezra Pound, and Edmund Wilson.

Letter to Anaïs Nin (March 1934):

> . . . I also reserved *Sanctuary* by Faulkner. I have a feeling that he is the only possible rival I have today in America. I am very curious to read him. (*Henry Miller: Letters to Anais Nin.*, ed. Gunther Stuhlmann, 130).

> Hemingway in my mind was not the great writer they make him out to be. He was a craftsman. But he wasn't a craftsman as good as Somerset Maughm [*sic*]. . . . And I must tell you, as much as I put him down, that first book, *The Sun Also Rises*, had a lot to do with my going to France, it inspired me to go. It shows something, doesn't it? (*Conversations with Henry Miller*, eds. Frank Keisnowski and Alice Hughes. (220–22 *passim*).

Dorothy Parker (1893–1967)

Her trenchant wit at the Algonquin Round Table earned her Alexander Woollcott's quip that she was "a blend of little Nell and Lady Macbeth." She was also a short-story writer, a poet, and a drama critic for *Vanity Fair* and *The New Yorker*.

With the possible exception of Ring Lardner, he [Hemingway] is less the literary character-part than any writer I have ever known. . . . He works like hell, and through it. Nothing comes easy to him; he struggles, sets down a word, scratches it out, and begins all over. He regards his art as hard and dirty work, with no hope of better conditions." (Dorothy Parker: "The Artist's Reward," a "Profile" in *The New Yorker*, November 30, 1929, 29).

Parker ends her profile reflecting on Hemingway's response to a query about what he understood by 'guts' : "I mean," Hemingway said, "grace under pressure." And Parker adds, "That grace is his. The pressure, I suppose, comes in gratis, under the heading of the Artist's Reward" (31). In a letter to Robert Benchley (Nov. 7, 1929), Parker had complained that Hemingway had agreed to the interview only on the condition that there be no mention of his Oak Park family or his divorce from Hadley.

Parker was either unaware of, or chose to ignore Hemingway's nasty poem, "To a Tragic Poetess—Nothing in her life became her like her almost leaving it," (*Ernest Hemingway: 88 Poems*, ed. Nicholas Gero-giannis, 90) which alludes mockingly to Parker's attempts at suicide. Hemingway seems to have been deeply affronted by Parker's dislike of Spain and disgust with bullfights.

Separated from Hadley and awaiting Pauline's return to Paris, he insisted on reciting the poem at a party at the MacLeishes over vigorous objections by Donald Ogden Stewart—which may have initiated the break-up of that particular friendship. (Marion Meade, *Dorothy Parker: What Fresh Hell Is This?*, 173).

Parker was also friendly with Faulkner, meeting him with some frequency in New York, where she introduced him to the Algonquin group, as well as in Hollywood.

Josephine Herbst (1897–1969)

Herbst and her husband John Herrmann, both novelists, met Hemingway in Paris in the 1920s and renewed their friendship in Greenwich Village and Key West (where Hemingway humiliated Herrmann during a fishing trip during the 1930s). Herbst and Hemingway were in Spain together during the Civil War where she became embroiled in the fracas that ensued there between Dos Passos (see Dos Passos above) and Hemingway. That she could maintain objectivity toward Hemingway as an artist is extraordinary considering his treatment of her husband (she threatened to shoot Hemingway unless he stopped) and his snide ambivalence toward her bisexuality.

[1927: "A Year of Disgrace"]:

> Mobility not only was in the blood but was a fact. The youthful juices had neither jellied nor atrophied, and if some of the young played with the recklessness of a gambler, with no more of a stake than talent and a fanatic's will, if the risks were high, what did you lose? . . . It was in this kind of setting that the early stories of Hemingway—then playing a lone hand in Paris—made so grave a mark. His young Nick might be the remains of the solitary trapper, but now he was educated, and through with everything, nourishing the residual grit of anarchism as a last hope. . . . It was really honest. Don't be sentimental and hold on to something that is dead. Beat it. (Josephine Herbst, *The Starched Blue Sky of Spain and Other Memoirs*, 72).

1936, Madrid:

> He had answered a definite call when he came to Spain. He wanted to be *the* war writer of his age, and he knew it and went

toward it. War gave answers that could not be found in that paradise valley of Wyoming . . . or even in the waters of Key West.
. . . What was the deepest reality *there* was in an extreme form
here and he knew it.

He was a real friend to the Spanish; he had donated an ambulance and had come as a correspondent. He was promoting the
film The Spanish Earth. . . . But in annexing new realms of experience, Hemingway was entering into some areas that were better
known to people like Dos Passos or even myself. He seemed to
be naively embracing on the simpler levels the current ideologies
at the very moment when Dos Passos was urgently questioning
them. . . . (Herbst, 150–51).

Glenway Wescott (1901–87)

. . . there was Ernest Hemingway, who was immensely good-
looking, animated, and hardworking. The French used to say he
had esprit—a rather light, pointed, and quotable way of talking.
He was, I believe, an incredible genius, but he was never a very
happy one, nor a very intelligent one. He had a bad tongue, and
he more than once used it to play mean tricks on me. . . . [See
Sylvia Beach, above].

Certain traits of his character . . . a lack of perception of causes
and effects in human nature and behavior, and, in consequence,
some sentimentality and occasional wild lapses into melo-
drama—kept him from ever writing an altogether first-rate
novel. Consequently, his short stories are better than his novels
. . . These are nuggets of pure experience set apart from all the
matrix of the world. (Glenway Wescott, "Foreword" to Hugh
Ford, *Four Lives in Paris, xvi–xvii*).

Kay Boyle (1902–92)

Coming from Minnesota, Boyle lived in France from the 1920s until World War II and knew most of the aspiring writers through her friendship with Robert McAlmon [see above]. In later years, she revised his *Being Geniuses Together* (1939; rev. 1968), adding alternate chapters recording her own memories of those French years. A prolific stylist, Boyle wrote novels, short stories, poetry, and essays. She was a foreign correspondent for *The New Yorker* and, in her later years, taught at San Francisco State University and became a fixture in the San Francisco literary scene.

Asked whether something special characterized the 1920s:

> There was indeed. It was the revolt against all literary pretentiousness, against weary, dreary rhetoric, against all the outworn literary and academic conventions. Our slogans were Down with Henry James, down with Edith Wharton, down with the sterility of "The Waste Land" . . .
>
> We had certain idols . . . Joyce, of course, and the short stories of Sherwood Anderson. We hailed the true simplicity of the early work of Hemingway . . . And of course there was Gertrude Stein. Without Gertrude Stein there might not have been as articulate a Sherwood Anderson and, undoubtedly, really undoubtedly, there would have been a less disciplined Hemingway. . . . ("Kay Boyle—Paris Wasn't like That," an interview with Leo Litwak, the *New York Times Book Review*, July 15, 1984, 32).

Writing to Waverley Root (c. December, 1932), who had criticized McAlmon's inclusion in the CCE (Crosby Continental Editions) by comparing him with Hemingway, Kay Boyle insisted that McAlmon was owed " 'a debt of influence' as the 'sound and almost heedless builder of a certain strong wind in American letters' and Hemingway 'as the gentleman who came in afterward and laid down the linoleum because it was so easy to keep clean.'" (Hugh Ford, *Published in Paris*, 226.)

The 1940s

TEN YEARS AFTER the onset of the Great Depression, the world once more found itself engulfed in war, this time global in scope and, especially in its earlier stages, precipitously in danger of becoming overwhelmed by what appeared to be the Axis crusade against civilization. Hemingway and Faulkner, still relatively young men in their early forties, still professionally and personally ambitious, sought somehow to express, whether in their lives or their writing, some sense of the significance of this terrible time—a time for them, like all humanity, to confront the nightmare of mortality.

Hemingway's only novel in this decade, *For Whom the Bell Tolls*, appeared in 1940, but although it undeniably sided against the Fascists, its voice remained characteristically Hemingway's—that of the individual struggling against a hostile world. Acting nominally as a war correspondent, Hemingway reported military actions on various fronts for newspapers and magazines, and, true to the defiant self-image he had fashioned into and through the 1930s, took an active role in combat situations—using his boat, the *Pilar*, as an anti-submarine vessel in the Caribbean, accompanying RAF missions from England, reporting from a landing craft on the GIs disembarkment at Normandy on D day, riding in the vanguard of the troops which entered Paris, and enduring some of the worst days of the campaign in the Huertgen Forest with the 22nd Infantry Regiment. For the rest of the decade, he established his home base at the Finca Vigia with his fourth wife, Mary Welsh, making visits to Ketchum, Idaho, and Venice.

On his part, after several futile attempts to join the Naval Air Force, Faulkner spent most of the war years shuttling between Hollywood and Oxford, Mississippi, writing scripts, worrying constantly over unpaid bills, and establishing a lethal pattern of alcoholic collapse and recovery. It was also at this time that he conceived and commenced work on what he believed would be his masterpiece, *The Fable*. Nevertheless, Faulkner produced other memorable work. Besides *Intruder in the Dust* (1948), he continued to work on his sequels to *The Hamlet* (1940) which would become his Snopes trilogy in the 1950s. And in *Go Down, Moses* (1942), he engaged directly the racial dilemma that had obsessed him profoundly since *The Sound and the Fury* (1929). Nowhere, possibly, has he probed that issue more dramatically or more nobly than in "The Bear," which tests interracial linkages, considers the implications of the perennial quest for the father, and gives lyric expression to the inexorable conflict as well as the bond between man and nature. In what was eventually to cause a major turnaround in Faulkner's financial situation, as well as a catapult to his reputation, Malcolm Cowley's *The Viking Portable Faulkner* (1946) re-introduced his work to the greater public.

Dashiell Hammett (1894–1961)

In a letter (April 14, 1931) to Lillian Hellmann, Hammett wrote that *Sanctuary* had "a nice taste for the morbid and gruesome," although it was "overrated" (*Selected Letters of Dashiell Hammett*, eds. Richard Layman with Julie M. Rivett, 70).

"He was jealous of Faulkner even as he enjoyed the companionship of a writer toward whom he could not feel superior. For Hemingway, whose . . . prose style he was said to have imitated, he professed no use at all: 'Hemingway sees himself as Hercules astride a woman,' (he) told Lily (Hellmann). . . ." (Joan Mellen, *Hellmann and Hammett: The Legendary Passion of Lillian Hellmann and Dashiell Hammett*, 51).

Hellmann (1905–84), on the other hand, commented after Hemingway's death: "He was a wonderful writer. I read proof on his first book when I was a 20-year-old at Horace Liveright. *In Our Time*, his first collection of short stories came in as a manuscript, and I remember the great joy of taking it home that first night. I still think it was his best book." (*New York Times*, July 3, 1961).

Thornton Wilder (1897–1975)

Wilder and Hemingway met at Sylvia Beach's bookstore shortly before the publication of *The Sun Also Rises* and thereafter maintained a cordial yet guarded friendship, each finding polite but cogent reason not to accept the other's invitations to meet except casually. Wilder, who admired Faulkner's work enormously, contrived to meet him while Faulkner was in Boston trying to shape *Requiem for a Nun* into a playable theater piece. Faulkner deliberately and cruelly went into his "super Southern country boy routine" so frustrating Wilder's efforts at intelligent discourse about Faulkner's work that Wilder later concluded that Faulkner hated him. Wilder was undoubtedly wrong; Faulkner simply found Wilder too literary, too intellectual. (Blotner, *Faulkner, a Biography*, 2, 1401–1402).

About *Light in August* (Williamsburg, Virginia, April 10, 1940):

So much that is splendid, but finally swamped and defeated in the emotional steam, the drive to cruelty, the confusion as to

what is good and bad, the mix-up that arises from identifying
the strong with the good, and the gentle with the bad. The image
of the South, crying out in self-justification and self-condemna-
tion, and all twisted by bitterness. . . . There is something very
adolescent about W.F.'s preoccupation with the sexual life of his
characters: Balzac must tell the financial status of each of his
characters; W.F. must tell how they spend their nights—and particularly adolescent is the recurrent necessity to inquire into
how they *first* knew sex. (*The Journals of Thornton Wilder,
1939–1961*, selected and edited by Donald Gallup, 18–19).

Dawn Powell (1897–1965)

Dawn Powell came to New York from Ohio in 1916 and seems to
have known everyone who lived in or came briefly to visit New York
City between 1920 and 1950. She met Faulkner on several occasions
and established warm friendships with John Dos Passos and Edmund
Wilson. She may have first met Hemingway in Greenwich Village in
1925 through her friendship with Josephine Herbst (Mellow, 326).
Powell was also well acquainted with Pauline Pfeiffer's sister, Virginia,
and Gerald and Sara Murphy. In her novels, *Turn, Magic Wheel* (1936)
and *A Time to Be Born* (1942), the character, Andrew Callingham, is
modeled somewhat on Hemingway.

He [EH] called Dawn Powell a wonderful writer who "has everything that Dotty Parker is supposed to have and is not tear-
stained." (Lillian Ross, *Portrait of Hemingway* [with a new
Afterword by the author], 69–70).

Letter to John Dos Passos (June 8, 1937). On the second conference
of the American Writers' Congress:

Ernest gave a good speech if that's what you like and his sum
total was that war was pretty nice and a lot better than sitting
around a hot hall and writers ought to all go to war and get killed
and if they didn't they were a big sissy. Then he went over to the
Stork Club. Followed by a pack of foxes. (*Selected Letters of
Dawn Powell*, ed., Tim Page, 98).

Letter to Max Perkins (Summer 1940):

I have yet to see anyone around Ernest even a few minutes who
is not violently affected by him, as you say. He probably has
more sheer personal power—I doubt if it's 'charm'—than anyone I ever met. Maybe Hitler is like that. Anyway, around him
it is hard to remember there is anyone else you planned to see
or ever cared to. I think people will have to get ernest-proofed
first, in order to hang on to their original prejudices when talking to him. (*Letters*, 108).

Jan. 2, 1941:

The avoidance of contemporary manners in contemporary writing... O'Hara writes of one small section of 52 St. or Broadway.
We have Hemingway, who writes of a fictional novel hero in
Spain with the language neither Spanish nor English. *(The Diaries of Dawn Powell: 1931–1965*, ed. Tim Page, 188).

Feb. 7, 1944:

... Letter from Hemingway very cheering. Said I was his favorite
living writer. (*Diaries*, 226).

Jan. 25, 1954:

Hemingway and his wife lost in Africa plane crash.... By Mon-
day they were found and his sales has another jolt upward. ...

But perhaps his real death will be unmarked, unnoticed. I tried once again to read Farewell to Arms and it seems as clumsily written as ever to me, like Walter Scott, difficult reading, pidgin English. (*Diaries*, 332).

May 24, 1965:

> . . . (Carlos) Baker writes [that Hemingway] refers to Sara (Murphy), Granny [Grantland Rice (1880–1954), a distinguished sportswriter and a poet whose column, "The Sportlight" was nationally syndicated] and me as his best friends. I feel like writing something about him as so many detractors are around. There was the unappreciated fact that he spread excitement and glamour wherever he appeared. (*Diaries*, 472).

John Steinbeck (1902–68)

In the spring of 1944, when Hemingway expressed an interest in meeting Steinbeck, a small party was arranged at Tim Costello's Bar on Third Avenue in New York City. Included among the participants were Vincent Sheean, John Hersey, and Steinbeck with their respective wives, and Robert Capa, Costello, John O'Hara, and Hemingway. Apparently, as often happens when significant writers are arbitrarily brought together, Steinbeck and Hemingway had little to say to one another. The one memorable incident, accompanied by heavy drinking, in fact, focused on a walking stick—a gift from Steinbeck to O'Hara, which the latter had proudly displayed as a genuine blackthorn. Hemingway challenged its authenticity, betting fifty dollars that he could split it over his head—which, in fact, he did, leaving O'Hara humiliated and Steinbeck bemused at what he felt to be Hemingway's gratuitous cruelty. (Benson, 547–48)

After reading "The Killers":

> ... this "was the finest writer alive. (Jackson J. Benson, *The True Adventures of John Steinbeck, Writer*, 156). Fearful of being over-influenced, Steinbeck said that he resisted reading any Hemingway through the 1930s.

A friend's recollection of an afternoon in Steinbeck's apartment:

> He [Steinbeck] would suddenly put down the bowl of onions he was peeling for the great chili he used to make. "Hemingway," he'd sneer, although nobody had mentioned Hemingway, and he would get up and go over and take *The Sun Also Rises* from a bookshelf. Then, sighing with satisfaction, he would read aloud, intoning the celebrated dialogue in a deliberately flat voice, without cadence, without caesura, and naturally it sounded awful. Then, pursing his lips and nodding, he would close the book and slap it against his knee. "God damn it. I don't understand why people think Hemingway can write dialogue." And for a little while he would be happy. (Benson, 548–49).

Letter of September 10, 1952:

> Just read Hemingway's new book (*The Old Man and the Sea*). A very fine performance. I am so glad. The obscene joy with which people trampled him on the last one was disgusting. Now they are falling too far the other way almost in shame. (Benson, 730).

Steinbeck's initial meeting with Faulkner (January, 1955) was almost as unpleasant as his encounter with Hemingway. Dreading the engagement, which included the Steinbecks, Faulkner's editor, Saxe

Cummings, and Jean Stein (Faulkner's girlfriend), Faulkner arrived for pre-dinner cocktails already thoroughly drunk, and his conversation throughout the evening consisted of a series of laconic responses and grunts. Later, he apologized and the two writers were able to maintain a social cordiality as long as they avoided "talking about themselves, other writers, or literature." (Benson, 770).

Letter to James S. Pope (May 16, 1956):

> A letter . . . today enclosed an interview with Bill Faulkner which turns my stomach. When those old writing boys get to talking about the Artist, meaning themselves, I want to leave the profession . . . THE ARTIST—my ass! Sure he's a good writer but he's turning into a god damned phoney. (*Steinbeck: A Life in Letters*, eds. Elaine Steinbeck and Robert Wallston, 529).

Letter to Pascal Covici, July 1961:

> The first thing we heard of Ernest Hemingway's death was a call . . . asking me to comment on it . . . I find it shocking. He had only one theme—only one. A man contends with the forces of the world, called fate, and meets them with courage. Surely a man has a right to remove his own life but you'll find no such possibility in any of H's heros [*sic*]. . . . But apart from all that—he has had the most profound effect on writing—more than anyone I can think of. He has not a vestige of humor. . . . Always he tried to prove something . And you only try to prove what you aren't sure of. He was the critics' darling because he never changed style, theme, nor story. He made no experiments in thinking nor in emotion. . . . I am saddened at his death . . . he

was always pleasant and kind to me although I am told that privately he spoke very disparagingly of my efforts. But then he thought of other living writers, not as contemporaries but as antagonists. (Steinbeck and Wallston, 703–705).

After being awarded the Nobel Prize, Steinbeck was asked who were his favorite authors

Faulkner and Hemingway, he said. Hemingway's short stories and nearly everything Faulkner wrote. (Benson, 915).

Hamilton Basso (1904–64)

A New Orleans–born novelist, biographer, and journalist (long-time associate editor of *The New Yorker*), Basso originally met Faulkner as part of the Sherwood Anderson circle in New Orleans, and later in New York City. Assigned by the magazine to do a profile on Faulkner, he agreed to respect the latter's request for privacy.

. . . all a writer's best characters . . . are reflections . . . of himself. Getting down to people I've actually known, Scott Fitzgerald was certainly a person out of one of his books; Gatsby, I would say, more than anyone else. Thomas Wolfe . . . is an obvious example. Hemingway, who is something of a mess, seems to have decided that his whole life should be led in imitation of his fiction. Sherwood Anderson was one of those half-articulate, muggy-minded people that turn up in Winesburg and Edmund Wilson . . . is one of the old natives of Hecate County. . . . Dreiser was Sister Carrie's big brother and . . . O'Neill . . . could be a figure waiting in the wings for his cue in a play by Eugene

O'Neill—the tragic life thrice compounded. (From "Notes of an interview for *The New Yorker* pieces, "The Tragic Sense," *The New Yorker*, February 28, March 6, March 13, 1948. Quoted in Louis Sheaffer, *O'Neill: Son and Artist*, (600–601).

John O'Hara (1905–70)

Letter to John Steinbeck (June 2, 1949):

> Writing. You and Ernest and Faulkner only. Me, of course. But room for all of us . . . You know that the one is Faulkner, the genius. You are closer to him than Ern or I. Fitzgerald was a better just plain writer than all of us put together. Just words writing. But he dade. The working men are you and I. Faulkner, there is nobody like little Willie. Ern has become the modern sym—something for writing and knows it. (Cited in Frank Mac-Shane, *The Life of John O'Hara*, 132).

Letter to William Maxwell (September 23, 1960). In defense of the notorious review of *Across the River* in the *New York Times Book Review* (September 10, 1950) in which O'Hara asserted that Hemingway was "the outstanding author since the death of Shakespeare":

> We start with a first-rate, original, conscientious artist, who caught on because of his excellence. The literary and then the general public very quickly realized that a great artist was functioning in our midst . . . his name is a synonym for writing with millions of people who have never read any work of fiction. (MacShane, 153).

Hemingway, in turn, manages the last (posthumous) word on their relationship:

> . . . I thought of O'Hara, fat as a boa constrictor that had swallowed an entire shipment of a magazine called Collier's and surly as a mule that had been bitten by tsetse flies plodding along dead without recognizing it. (*True At First Light*, ed. Patrick Hemingway, 233).

Richard Wright (1908–60)

Wright's sensational novel, *Native Son* (1940), based in part on an actual case about two killings committed by a black man, stirred readers and, a year later, stage audiences in a version produced by Orson Welles. Five years later, by then a member of the Communist Party, Wright published the autobiography *Black Boy*. Addressing the rage expressed in that work, William Faulkner wrote the author that the book said well what deserved saying, but not so well as in *Native Son*. What really matters for an artist, Faulkner advises, is that "the good lasting stuff come out of one individual's imagination and sensitivity to and comprehension of the suffering of Everyman. Anyman, not out of the memory of his own grief." (*Selected Letters of William Faulkner*, 201). Wright's angry portrait of racial injustice accompanied his long commitment to Communism, but by 1950, when he left the United States forever, he wrote, in a chapter of *The God that Failed*, about his disillusionment with the Communist Party. From his permanent residence in Paris, Wright continued to inveigh against injustice, his rage too often ill-controlled, but always unsettling, even threatening, as in the collection of essays called *White Man, Listen!* (1957).

I [Margaret Walker] think from the beginning (Spring, 1936) we differed about Hemingway and Faulkner. Although I had read some of Hemingway, I had not read much of Faulkner, and despite Wright's ecstatic feeling about *Sanctuary*, I found it revolting. . . . (Margaret Walker, *Richard Wright: Daemonic Genius*, 74).

Wright was very fond of Hemingway's action-filled and violent stories. He studied the laconic style of Hemingway's lean prose cut to a bare minimum . . . and comparing it to the involuted page-long sentences and paragraphs of William Faulkner, Wright sought to imitate the best of both. (Walker, 256).

William Saroyan (1908–81)

A blithe Californian spirit, Saroyan wrote (often with excessive sentiment) of his love for all humanity. In fact, despite the lovable folk drawn from his native Fresno—the characters in his Pulitzer Prize play, *The Time of Your Life* (1939) and his novel *The Human Comedy* (1943)—he was himself nasty, belligerent, and cruel to family, friends, and fellow artists. His first collection of stories, *The Daring Young Man on the Flying Trapeze* (1934), won him immediate fame and Hemingway's wrath when he mocked *Death in the Afternoon*, comparing it to "a great philosophical work on tennis." Despite tempering his ridicule with admiration for Hemingway's prose, Saroyan could not escape Hemingway's threat to "push your puss in." After the liberation of Paris in 1945, Hemingway, Saroyan, and their friends tangled in a restaurant brawl instigated by Hemingway's reference to Saroyan as "a lousy Armenian son of a bitch." The police were called and all the participants were, as a witness attested, "thrown *up* the

stairs and into the Paris blackout . . . Ernest was laughing like a
hyena." (Baker, *Life*, 442).

On Hemingway's suicide:

> I would be embarrassed . . . by such a violent suicide as poor Mr.
> Hemingway's. I speak with tremendous sympathy and under-
> standing of the predicament of a man who can no longer endure
> himself . . . a failure of his identity. . . . [He] equated reality with
> a continuation of his posey writing, and by posey I mean that
> hero character he invented, which the whole world would love
> and be influenced by it, couldn't be continued. I don't want to
> call Hem a dishonest writer, but essentially this is a fantasy
> writer. (Garig Basmadjian, "Candid Conversation, 25 May,
> 1975), in *William Saroyan: The Man and the Writer Remem-
> bered*, ed., Leo Hamalian, 144).

[Interview] "Did he Influence You?":

> Never! The New Testament and the Old Testament did much
> more than he did . . . the guy who influenced me more than
> Hemingway ever did . . . Sherwood Anderson. I love Sherwood.
> I've written tributes to Sherwood, but I won't write a tribute to
> Hemingway as a writer, because first of all he'd like to feel that
> he influenced everybody . . . Hemingway is a great, great stylist
> . . . it would be dishonest to say I was unaware of his writing.
> Aware and respectful of its effectiveness. But I hated *For Whom
> the Bell Tolls*. I couldn't read it. ("Candid Conversation," 144).

Nelson Algren (1909–81)

Possibly because he was a fellow-Chicagoan, Hemingway was un-
characteristically complimentary of Algren's work and entertained

him at Finca Vigia. He provided the following blurb for *The Man with the Golden Arm* which Doubleday chose not to use: "Into a world of letters where we have the fading Faulkner and that overgrown Lil Abner Thomas Wolfe casts a shorter shadow every day, Algren comes like a corvette or even a big destroyer when one of those things is what you need and need it badly and at once and for keeps. . . . Algren can hit with both hands and move around and he will kill you if you are not awfully careful. . . . Mr. Algren, boy, you are good." (Hemingway to Algren, 1949, Ohio State University Division of Rare Books and Manuscripts; cited in Bettina Drew, *Nelson Algren: A Life on the Wild Side*, 210).

The only things that last are the things that are done when the writer doesn't know what he's doing—that kind of innocence. Faulkner didn't really know what he was doing . . . because he was working out of a compulsion. He didn't know and he certainly would have defended himself against having it broken down. He knew that much about it. He had a drive. Certainly, Hemingway, in this sense, never knew what he was doing. (*Conversations with Nelson Algren*, ed. H. E. F. Donahue, 132). Cited in Drew, *Algren*, (203).

Wright Morris (1910–98)

Although he lived most of his life in California, and traveled widely in Europe and Mexico, Morris's reputation is rooted in the Nebraska plains where he was born and spent his childhood. Despite H. L. Mencken's sneering comment about the fiction of an earlier Nebraskan, Willa Cather ("I don't care how well she writes. I don't give a damn what happens in Nebraska"), Morris, like Cather, never stopped caring and, staying within the prairie tradition he knew best, shaped more than thirty books—novels, short stories, memoirs, essays, and photographs—many of them penetrating studies of the less than tranquil lives of prairie dwellers. In one of them, *The Field of Vision* (1956), a Mexican bullfight compels a group of midwesterners to face their own moments of truth.

Citing Mark Twain and Gertrude Stein as pioneers who challenged readers by compelling their concentration on style, Morris continues:

> . . . disarming vernacular comes out of Huck Finn but it was Gertrude Stein who revealed to Hemingway the wider range of its possibilities. Through Hemingway, the virus of the vernacular spread world-wide. (Wright Morris, *About Fiction*, 14).

On Hemingway's mockery of Sherwood Anderson's style in *Torrents of Spring*:

> His [Hemingway's] own voice is so marked, however, we cannot detect the voice he hoped to ridicule. *The Torrents of Spring* is a parody of Hemingway by Hemingway. (*About Fiction*, 129).

In "A Reader's Sampler," from *About Fiction*, Morris cites twenty works of "great fiction" commenting briefly on each:

In Our Time (1924):

> The captivity of Hemingway's style still sends men on safaris, gives tone to war and murder, comforts the loser, and draws trout from the streams of our imagination. . . . He was the first to grasp that overlarge expectations give rise to bad losers, and

that grace under pressure is the bullfighter's option, not the bull's. (157).

On *Red Leaves* (1930):

The spectacle of human folly gives rise in Faulkner, as it did to Twain, to outbursts of mythic humor. The frontier provides the landscape for this humor, which is often at the heart of a wilderness. Twain had his Territory Ahead, Faulkner his tribe of fabulous Indians. (161).

The 1950s

POST-WORLD WAR II found a somewhat muddled America with a radically altered geopolitical landscape—one in which its dominant military and economic power was shadowed by the threat of nuclear catastrophe. For good and for bad, it was now permanently global in its presence in world affairs—The Marshall Plan, the Korean Conflict, the heating up of the "Cold War" which would ignite small and large regional upheavals in Asia, Africa, and Central America for the next thirty years. Institutions such as the Voice of America, the USIA open libraries, and the Fulbright Exchange Programs were introducing American art and literature to people all over the world. On the domestic scene, released from the austerity of the war years, there was unparalleled prosperity; a major surge in educational possibilities with the G.I. Bill and, later, the National Defense Education Act (1958); the horrendous backlash of reactionary militancy in McCarthyism; and the significant progressive ruling of the Supreme Court that segregation by color was a violation of the 14th Amendment. Television, which was eventually to change reading habits in a major way, had effectively replaced radio as a national news and entertainment source, bringing, among other commodities, Elvis Presley and the beginnings of what was to become an explosively commercialized "youth culture."

And perhaps more personally relevant to Hemingway and Faulkner and their self-images, a new generation of writers was emerging who had casually absorbed or rejected the influences of the two older novelists. Among others, Norman Mailer's *The Naked and the Dead* (1948) and James Jones's *From Here to Eternity* (1951) attempted to do for war fiction what Hemingway had done in *A Farewell to Arms*. William Styron's *Lie Down in Darkness* (1951) showed how thoroughly the Faulknerian influence had entered the wordstream of younger writers. And the appearances of J. D. Salinger's *Catcher in the Rye* (1952), Ralph Ellison's *Invisible Man* (1952), and Saul Bellow's third novel, *The Adventures of Augie March* (1953) announced the arrival of new talents, eager, as artists inevitably are, to take over the mantles of their predecessors. And in an anointment which is often accompanied by a valedictorian air, Stockholm awarded Nobel Prizes to both writers—Faulkner in 1949 and Hemingway in 1954.

Both men continued to produce considerable work. Hemingway published the last two novels which would appear in his lifetime, the almost unanimously derided *Across the River and Into the Trees* (1950) and the impressive novella, *The Old Man and the Sea* (1952)—a kind of summary of the themes that had animated his work from the outset: love and death and loneliness, courage, and a vague but irrepressible hope for renewal. As usual, his non-literary adventures elicited headlines around the world, as when his successive airplane crashes in Africa left him with a ruptured spleen and kidney, as well as damage to his spine. Yet, during the physically and mentally painful last years of his life, he labored at his desk, assembling the fascinating memoir of Paris in the 1920s that would appear posthumously as *A Moveable Feast* (1964), as well as working on the materials that became *Islands in the Stream* (1970), *The Garden of Eden* (1986), and *True At First Light* (1999).

Despite his own struggles with alcoholism, depression, and severe anxiety, Faulkner also sought to assuage his pain in hard work. In the latter part of the decade, he completed the chronicle of the Snopes family that he had begun in 1940 (*The Hamlet*) with *The Town* (1957) and *The Mansion* (1959). But the major work of this period is *A Fable* (1954). Ten years in the writing, this was to be his masterpiece. As he confessed once, this was his only major piece of writing where he did not do a whirlwind first draft; instead he returned again and again to the manuscript, replacing visions with revisions, encumbering perhaps the structural and allegorical intricacies of the novel in its own sluggish verbiage. Nevertheless, as with the bulk of his work, *A Fable* resonates with his unshakable faith in the resilience of the human spirit, or, as noted in his earlier Nobel Prize speech: "I believe that man will not merely endure: he will prevail."

James Thurber (1894–1961)

Postscript to a letter to Katherine White (February 23, 1938):

> I have decided that the Little Man, the bewildered man, the nervous, beaten, wife-crossed man, is a realer and stronger thing in American life than . . . the Hemingway men that choke guys to death. (*The Thurber Letters*, ed. Harrison Kinney with Rosemary A. Thurber, 280).

> [c. 1957] . . . the characteristic fear of the American writer . . . is the process of aging. The writer looks in the mirror and examines his hair and teeth to see if they're still with him. "Oh my God," he says, "I wonder how my writing is. I bet I can't write

today." The only time I met Faulkner he told me he wanted to live long enough to do three more novels. He was fifty-three then, and I think he has done them. Then Hemingway says, you know, that he doesn't expect to be alive after sixty. . . . When I met Hemingway with John O'Hara in Costello's Bar . . . we sat around and talked about how old we were getting. . . . I've never known a woman who could weep about her age the way the men I know can. ("James Thurber," *Writers at Work: Paris Review Interviews, First Series*, ed. George Plimpton, 97–98. See also, below, Lillian Ross).

Malcolm Cowley (1898–1989)

On being questioned as to which of his critical pieces gave him satisfaction (March 5, 1981), Cowley said: ". . . Faulkner, yes, that would be one. But also I helped at other stages to bring together a consideration of the World War I generation as something that had to be considered apart. Its story made a sort of collective novel. I think that was good. I think the first essay I did on Hemingway was a very good one and changed the whole direction of Hemingway criticism. I think the Faulkner Portable changed the direction of Faulkner criticism . . . These are moments I like to remember. . . ." ("Day of Doom, Day of Dreams: Malcolm Cowley on the 1930s," Interview by Philip L. Gerber and Joan Rubin, *Horns of Plenty*, 50).

Cowley's high-school classmate in Pittsburgh, Kenneth Burke (1897–1993) never completed college and had few readers beyond academic circles despite his output of a dozen books, including poetry and fiction as well as his central concern, literary criticism. He taught at various colleges, chiefly at Bennington, joined with Ransom, Tate, and others to found the New Criticism, and earned praise from W. H. Auden, Harold Bloom, and Denis Donoghue as one of America's most brilliant critics and literary theorists.

Letter from Kenneth Burke to Malcolm Cowley (October 3, 1929):

> I do not have so strongly as you the test of naturalness in writing—for it leads too inexorably to Hemingway, whom I hate as though sent upon earth to hate him. . . . There is no particular virtue attached to naturalness, except where it is a hit, where the naturalness is exceptional in its enlightenment. (*The Selected Correspondence of Kenneth Burke and Malcolm Cowley: 1915– 1981*, ed. Paul Jay, 283).

Letter to Kenneth Burke (August 16, 1948):

> . . . as preparation for writing the piece in Life I have been writing a biography of Ernest from the cradle, not quite to the grave, and working up considerable admiration for the Great Man—as I told you, he pays the price for greatness, as if he went up to the cashier's desk after making his purchase; he pays the price by setting up a code for himself and living up to it, and by being extraordinarily attentive to everyone around him so they have to be attentive and admiring in return, just so that each of them can keep his self-respect. The interesting thing I discovered that he won't talk about is that he was a lonely and awkward boy bullied by his schoolmates, who were richer, better at sports, better liked by the girls. I think he's been revenging himself on his schoolmates for the last thirty-five years. He overcompensates—he started out by boasting and being a little bit of a four-flusher; now he does his boasting by indirection,

and if you call his four-flush you find it's a straight flush. (*Correspondence*, 190).

Letter from Kenneth Burke to Malcolm Cowley (February 22, 1963):

As for the Hemingway problem, I'd tentatively line it up thus: He worked up a love-and-war act. . . . There was a lotta shit implicit in the war side of that setup, and late on in life these implications began to make themselves more urgently felt. But being first of all a bully (as indicated by his love of bullfights), he kept being puzzled by the intuitive accuracy which brought him abreast of bullshit. So, when shit started coming out, he went back and tried starting over again. And if he did start over again and shit didn't transpire, he knew that that kind of development was somehow a lie, too. So, either way, he was caught. For his next phase required humility and/or humiliation for which his superb technique of bullying did not make allowance. (*Correspondence*, 346–47).

E. B. White (1899–1985)

Following *The New Yorker* tradition of parodies (Wolcott Gibbs's "Death in the Rumble Seat," October 8, 1932), White produced one of the most successful Hemingway send-ups in "Across the Street and into the Grill," *The New Yorker*, October 14, 1950.

Letter to Howard Cushman (June 21, 1967):

Most prose today, it seems to me, is not greatly different in style from the prose of our salad days. I've just read "The Secrets of Santa Vittoria"; except for a few passages that are more explicit than what was around in the Twenties, the book is straight going and derives from Hemingway, without H's lack of humor . . . All of us of our generation feel a great longing for the romanticism and the lyricism and the discipline of the writings that we cut our teeth on. (*Letters of E. B. White*, ed. Dorothy L. Guth, 551).

But in a later letter to William K. Zinsser (Dec. 30, 1968)—responding to a request to "assess" S. J. Perelman's work—White makes clear what he believes to be his own literary heritage:

I'm sure Sid's stuff influenced me in the early days . . . I don't like the word "humorist," never have. It seems to me misleading. Humor is a by-product that occurs in the serious work of some and not others. I was more influenced by Don Marquis than by Ernest Hemingway, by Perelman than by Dreiser . . . But if you're hoping to disabuse people of the notion that there is something vaguely second-rate about humorous expression in literature, I wish you luck. I don't think you have a prayer. (*Letters*, 574).

James T. Farrell (1904–79)

From "A Remembrance of Ernest Hemingway":

I met Ernest Hemingway in Key West in 1936. To me, he was very genial, friendly, and hospitable . . . One of the first things he said to me was that when he had read the fight scene in *Young Lonigan*, he had known that the writer had it, and knew what he was writing about. . . . (*Literary Essays*, ed. Jack Alan Robbins, 88).

Robert Penn Warren (1905–89)

Warren contributed to *The Fugitive* while he was still an undergraduate at Vanderbilt, and, in 1930, joined with a dozen others—including Allen Tate, Stark Young, and Donald Davidson—to sign that clarion call to Southern Agrarianism, social and political conservatism, *I'll Take My Stand*, a signature he later withdrew.

In 1946, Faulkner and Warren were simultaneously involved in one another's work: Faulkner reading and reporting enthusiastically (but wholly missing Warren's thematic center) about *All the King's Men* (see Letter to Lamont Davis, 25 July, 1946, *Selected Letters of William Faulkner*, ed. Joseph Blotner, 239) while Warren was preparing a review of Malcolm Cowley's *The Portable Faulkner* for *The New Republic*.

[c.1957] On Faulkner's technique of the "still moment":

That's the frozen moment. Freeze time . . . It's an important quality in his work. Some of these moments harden up an event, give it its meaning by holding it fixed. Time fluid versus time fixed. In Faulkner's work that's the drama behind the drama. Take a look at Hemingway; there's no time in Hemingway, there are only moments in themselves, moments of action. There are no parents and no children. If there's a parent he is a grandparent off in America somewhere who signs the check. . . . You never see a small child in Hemingway. You get death in childbirth but you never see a child. Everything is outside of the time process. But in Faulkner there are always the very old and the very young. Time spreads and is the important thing, the terrible thing . . . Everything is already there, just waiting to happen . . . These frozen moments are Faulkner's game. Hemingway has a different game. In Hemingway there's no time at all. He's out of history entirely. In one sense, he tries to deny history. ("Robert Penn Warren," *Writers at Work, First Series*, ed. George Plimpton, 201–2).

W. H. Auden (1907–73)

At the 1952 Paris meeting of the Congress for Cultural Freedom, Auden reported that "The Amerlogue writers contingent consisted of Katherine Anne [Porter] (who kept having heart attacks), Glenway Wescott . . . Allen Tate, Robert Lowell, me and Faulkner. We had an anxious time with the last for he went into a bout on arrival, shut up in his hotel throwing furniture out of the windows and bottles at the ladies and saying the most dreadful things about coons. However we managed to get him sober and onto the platform on the last day to say that the Americans had behaved badly but that he hoped they would behave better in the future and sit down." (Cited in Richard Davenport-Hines, *Auden!*, 280).

In an elegant review of Faulkner's *The Mansion*, the final volume of the Snopes trilogy, Auden dismissed as irrelevant claims that Faulkner was significant either as a thoughtful commentator on politics or race, an astute psychologist, or a master stylist. Instead, he focused on what he believed were the two salient talents that made Faulkner a great writer: his magical ability to "make twenty years in Yoknapatawpha seem . . . like twenty minutes;" and the ultimate moral purpose of his fiction which teaches the reader "to love the Good" and to recognize "the price that must be paid for that love." (*A Company of Readers*, ed. Arthur Krystal, 145–46).

Eudora Welty (1909–2001)

In 1943, entirely out of the blue, Welty was surprised to receive the following letter from Faulkner:

> Dear Welty: You are doing fine. You are doing all right. I read THE GILDED SIX BITS, a friend loaned me THE ROBBER BRIDEGROOM, I have just bought the collection named GREEN something, [*A Curtain of Green*, 1941] haven't read it yet . . . You are doing very fine. Is there any way I can help you? How old are you?
>
> When I read THE ROBBER BRIDEGROOM I thought of course of Djuna Barnes, the same as you thought of Djuna Barnes. I expect you to pass that, though. . . .
>
> Faulkner (27 April 1943).

As Joan St. C. Crane suggests, Faulkner was probably confusing Eudora Welty with Zora Lee Hurston, whose story, "The Gilded Six-Bits," appeared in the same August 1933 issue of *Story* Magazine as his own contribution, "Artist at Home." When Welty finally did meet Faulkner several years later, neither made any reference to the letter. (Joan St. C. Crane, "William Faulkner to Eudora Welty: A Letter," *The Mississippi Quarterly*, XLII:3, 223–26).

(c.1972) On the question of Faulkner's influence:

> I was naturally in the deepest awe and reverence of him. But that's no help in your own writing. Nobody can help you but yourself. So often I'm asked how I could have written a word with William Faulkner living in Mississippi, and this question amazes me. It was like living near a big mountain, something

majestic—it made me happy to know it was there, all that work of his life. But it wasn't a helping or hindering presence. Its magnitude, all by itself, made it something remote in my own working life. When I thought of Faulkner it was when I *read*. . . . ("Eudora Welty," *Writers at Work, Fourth Series*, ed. George Plimpton, 179–80).

Tennessee Williams (1911–83)

It was through *Cat [Cat on a Hot Tin Roof]* that I met Faulkner . . . we were there (Philadelphia, March, 1955) working on *Cat* . . . He never talked to me. I thought he disapproved of me. And then later that summer . . . (in Paris) all went to dinner together. I felt a terrible torment in the man. He always kept his eyes down. We tried to carry on a conversation but he would never participate. Finally, he lifted his eyes once in reponse to a direct question from me, and the look in his eyes was so terrible, so sad, that I began to cry. (Tennessee Williams, *Memoirs*, 170).

Mary McCarthy (1912–89)

Novelist, short-story writer, teacher, and, perhaps above all, a savage critic and often malicious satirist of the foibles of academics and other intellectuals (*The Groves of Academe*, 1952), and of women (*The Group*, 1963).

I hated Hemingway. He can go right in there with Lillian Hellmann. In fact, I think they'd make a wonderful pair; I think Hemingway is untruthful too. (*Conversations with Mary McCarthy*, ed. Carol Gelderman, 165).

Speaking about the difficulty of getting into Joyce's *Ulysses*:

> It was because . . . we had been reading diluted Joyce in writers
> like Faulkner and so had got used to his ways, at second remove.
> (Mary McCarthy, *Intellectual Memoirs: 1936–1938*, 25).

Delmore Schwartz (1913–66)

A man of diverse and exceptional talent, Schwartz was poet, critic,
editor, and teacher as well as writer of fiction. Despite his gifts, he
reveals in his work a tormented consciousness, pervasive guilt, and
an ironic tone of personal inadequacy—all eloquently manifest in
one of his finest stories, "In Dreams Become Responsibilities"
(1939). Schwartz served as a model for the hero in Saul Bellow's
Humboldt's Gift.

To Robert Hivnor (November 3, 1940):

> I read the new Hemingway novel (*For Whom the Bell Tolls*) and
> was almost persuaded; when the messenger goes back to the loy-
> alist lines the brotherhood of man becomes the bureaucracy of
> man and the book's morality is shown as inadequate. (*Letters of
> Delmore Schwartz*, selected and edited by Robert Phillips, 104).

Ralph Ellison (1914–94)

On Hemingway:

> . . . this was the Recession of 1937. . . . At night I practiced
> writing and studied Joyce, Dostoevski, Stein, and Hemingway.
> Especially Hemingway; I read him to learn his sentence struc-

ture and how to organize a story. I guess many young writers were doing this, but I also used his description of hunting when I went into the fields the next day. I had been hunting since I was eleven, but no one had broken down the process of wing-shooting for me, and it was from reading Hemingway that I learned to lead a bird. When he describes something in print, believe him; believe him even when he describes the process of art in terms of baseball or boxing; he's been there. ("Ralph Ellison," *Writers at Work. The Paris Review Interviews*, Second Series, ed. George Plimpton, 321).

Perhaps the discomfort about protest in books by Negro authors comes because since the nineteenth century American literature has avoided profound moral searching. It was too painful and besides there were specific problems of language and form to which the writers could address themselves. They did wonderful things, but perhaps they left the real problems untouched. There are exceptions, of course, like Faulkner who had been working the great moral theme all along, taking it up where Mark Twain put it down. ("Ellison," 333–34).

———

In a letter to Albert Murray (April 9, 1953), Ellison tells of his excitement at meeting Faulkner at Random House on the day of the National Book Award ceremony, admiring Faulkner's unexpectedly natty attire and delighting in his gracious acknowledgment that he had read *Invisible Man*. To Ellison's observation that Faulkner had "children all around now," Faulkner responded that he was "surprised to learn how many people like the stuff." (*Trading Twelves: The Selected Letters of Ralph Ellison and Albert Murray*, eds. Albert Murray and John F. Callahan, 44–45).

———

Letter to John Roche, (November 6, 1984):

> Those were days when the only way I could read a copy of The
> New York Times was by walking a mile or so from the Negro
> section into downtown Dayton—which I did daily so that I
> could read Hemingway's dispatches from the Spanish Civil War,
> which I studied for style as well as for information. . . . (*The New
> Republic*, March 1, 1999).

Flannery O'Connor (1925–84)

Letter to Sally and Robert Fitzgerald (January 25, 1953):

> I am sending you a subscription to something called the Shenan-
> doah. . . . I told them to bring it with the autumn issue that has
> a review of my book by . . . Brainard Cheney. It also has a review
> of The Old Man and the Sea by Wm. Faulkner, the review I
> mean, that is nice. He says that Hemingway discovered God the
> Creator in this one. What part I like in that was where the fish's
> eye was like a saint in a procession; it sounded to me like he was
> discovering something new maybe for him. (*The Habit of Being:
> Letters of Flannery O'Connor*, ed. Sally Fitzgerald, 56).

Letter to Father J. H. McCown (January 16, 1956):

> The Catholic fiction writer has very little high-powered 'Catho-
> lic' fiction to influence him except that written by these three
> (Bloy, Bernanos, and Mauriac), and Greene. But at some point
> reading them reaches the place of diminishing returns and you
> get more benefit reading someone like Hemingway, where there
> is apparently a hunger for Catholic completeness in life. (Fitz-
> gerald, 130).

Letter to "A" (March 20, 1958):

> Now about Joe Christmas. Joe Christmas is the hero of Faulk-
> ner's book *Light in August* which you had better get and read.
> It's a real sick-making book but I guess a classic. I read it a long
> time ago and only once so I am in no position to say. I keep clear
> of Faulkner so my own little boat won't get swamped. (Fitzger-
> ald, 273).

Letter to John Hawkes (July 27, 1958):

> I haven't written and thanked you for the books because I have
> been reading them. I braved the Faulkner, without tragic results.
> Probably the real reason I don't read him is because he makes
> me feel that with my one-cylinder syntax I should quit writing
> and raise chickens altogether. (Fitzgerald, 291–92).

Letter to "A" (October 14, 1961):

> I sort of distrust anybody's defining what the novel is or even
> isn't. . . . People have to use it for what they have to use it for,
> Hemingway had to test his manhood with it and V. Woolf had
> to make it a laboratory, and A. Huxley a place to give lectures
> in. . . . You can criticize what they had to do with it, but you've
> got to leave the form vague enough to include them in it. (Fitz-
> gerald, 451).

Lillian Ross (1927–   )

Having established friendly relations with Hemingway while re-
searching material on Sydney Franklin, the Brooklyn bullfighter,
Ross persuaded Hemingway to let her follow him around on a visit

to New York City. The resulting Profile in *The New Yorker*, "How Do You Like It Now, Gentlemen?" (May 13, 1950), presenting the writer as he shadow-boxed and pidgin-talked his way from the Plaza to Abercrombie & Fitch to the Metropolitan Museum, solidified for many readers an indelible image of the public Hemingway persona. Although Ross (and, less assuredly, Hemingway) felt that the portrait was a fair and essentially favorable depiction of the writer at his most ebulliently playful, many readers saw it as a scalpel-sharp hatchet job which ridiculed Hemingway as a man besotted in braggadocio and buffoonery. The Profile was reprinted with an additional Preface in *Portrait of Hemingway* (1961) and Ross reiterated her defense of the piece in *Reporting Back: Notes on Journalism* (2002). See, among others, Reynolds, *Hemingway: The Final Years*, 226–27.

On readers who thought the portrait satirical, driven by animosity, or devastatingly realistic, Ross writes: "[They] simply didn't like the way Hemingway talked; they didn't like his freedom; they didn't like his not taking himself seriously . . . they didn't like this and they didn't like that. In fact, they didn't like Hemingway to be Hemingway. . . . they couldn't understand his being a serious writer without being pompous." (from "The Preface," cited in *Reporting Back,* 146).

Among those readers seems to have been Alice B. Toklas: Letter to W. G. Rogers (Oct. 2, 1950): "Did you see the New Yorker's profile of Hemingway ???!!! Nothing he has said since—not even his novel—will be as complete an exposure of all he spent his life hiding. It's strange that he should be taking so much pleasure in destroying the legend he worked so patiently to construct." (*Letters of Alice B. Toklas: Staying on Alone*, ed. Edward Burns, 209).

And although Ross asserts that her *New Yorker* colleagues agreed with her assessment of the piece, James Thurber writes: "John Mc-

Nulty, who had this to say about Lillian Ross's Profile of Hemingway: 'It was like the Eddie Wakus [*sic*] affair—she loved him so much she shot him.'" (Harrison Kinney with Rosemary Thurber, eds., *The Thurber Letters*, 504–5).

Ramon Guthrie (1896–1973)

Awarded the Silver Star for his service in the nascent U.S. Army's Aviation Section in World War I, Guthrie returned to France after convalescence in the States, earned his *license* and *doctorat en droit*, then spent much of the next decade in France, painting, writing poetry and fiction, and translating from the Provençal. From 1930 until his retirement in 1963—except when he served with the O.S.S. in World War II—he was a full-time faculty member at Dartmouth College specializing in Marcel Proust. He seems to have remained on the fringes of the expatriate group as well as the larger body of at-home American poets, forging stronger relationships with Sinclair Lewis and some of the French artists, like the surrealist poet Robert Desnos, and Giacometti. In his last years, as his physical health deteriorated (cancer of the bladder and, subsequently, a removal of the colon), his poetic output exploded, both in quantity and quality. (See the Chronology in *Ramon Guthrie. Maximum Security Ward and Other Poems*, ed. Sally Gall, 205–10).

From " . . . For Approximately the Same Reason
   Why a Man Can't
   Marry His Widow's Sister"

The first time I saw him was at Stella's [Bowen],
rue Notre-Dame des Champs. Apple-cheeked manchild

right out of Satie's Enfance de Pantagruel.
Still married to Hadley. (Stella had just left Ford:
this party was to see if she herself
had any friends or if they all were Ford's.)

The last time I saw him was at
Robert Desnos' in the rue de Seine.
He wanted me to meet the ambulances at Le Havre
and smuggle them across the Pyrenees.
(I kept myself available, phoned every day;
nothing ever came of it.)

    . . .

Berlin. Ernest—not Papa for some years to come—
up from Paris to see the six-day bike race.
Pauline was this time's wife. Dinner with Red [Sinclair] Lewis.
A girl—Agatha?—prattled trilingually
of painters. Cézanne? Van Gogh? Picasso?
Juan Gris? Mais c'est a rire! Italians, yes.
But French, Spanish . . . Hemingway stood up and crashed
his fist down on the table. "El Greco is
   a cockeyed GOOD painter!"
The gnädige Fraulein squeaked and subsided mouselike.

   . . . can't marry his widow's sister . . .
12-gauge tranquilizer. At seven o'clock a Sunday morning . . .
having come through the night—and countless other nights.
How long had he been thinking of it? . . . 'me a failed
Catholic' . . . thinking in such terms
as how to pull the triggers?
   No longer apple-cheeked or cheeked at all.
   One WHITE silent bang where head had been ."
(Gall, ed., *Maximum Security Ward*, 160–162).

FIVE

The Exalted Larks

"Surely, if there are two professions in which there should be no professional jealousy, they are prostitution and literature."

William Faulkner, "On Criticism," *Double Dealer*, VII
(1925), 84

"It is almost as though they were fighting for billing on a tombstone."

John Steinbeck, cited in Jackson Benson, *The True Adventures of John Steinbeck, Writer*, 796

Hemingway on Faulkner; Faulkner on Hemingway

Curiously, Hemingway and Faulkner never met although their lives crossed tantalizingly close in Paris in the 1920s, in New York City, and in Hollywood. Two of their early poems appeared coincidentally in 1922 in the same issue of *The Double Dealer*, an avant-garde little magazine published in New Orleans. There is little doubt, however, that from their earliest publications each was acutely and intimately aware of the other's work and each recognized by the mid-1920s that the other was his chief rival for artistic eminence. Although, or perhaps because, each was an almost perfectly inverted mirror image of the other (even physically: Hemingway over six feet and a fleshy 200 pounds, Faulkner about five feet five, slender and trim), their competitive zeal ran deep and eventually, on Hemingway's part, grew bitter. Faulkner's lush volubility and Hemingway's sparse minimalism; Faulkner, courtly, private, stubborn, in some sense a fugitive in his own country; Hemingway, larger than life, a creature of the rotogravure sections, a gaudy public exile wherever he lived. Each respected, admired, and was somewhat nettled by the other's work, but each was militantly resolute to guard his own arduous path to literary excellence. Oddly enough, in their several semi-public exchanges, usually incited by misunderstandings of reported comments, it is the ostentatiously self-confident Hemingway who is quick to take umbrage and strike back at what he believed were Faulkner's criticisms of him and his work. During thirty-five years of toasting and taunting, Hemingway and Faulkner provided dramatic, if on occasion crude, flamboyant proof of what an entangled snake pit a literary milieu can be and how powerful are the profound urgencies that drive true creativity.

Let it be said at once: little of noble or profound utterance distinguishes the written give-and-take between Hemingway and Faulkner. What contemporary writers admired or abominated about the mysteries of their style or vision of life all too often resonates in the exchanges between them as little more than Hemingway's squawks of hurt pride and Faulkner's measured, patient, and sometimes naive efforts to explain his own position. The chronicle is more rewarding as it reveals human weakness than as it testifies to the growth and integrity of artistic consciousness. If, then, the account that follows disappoints expectations of significant intellectual discourse, one may nevertheless find lively evidence of both good and ill-nature, of awkward expression resulting in mutual misunderstanding, of unexpected bursts of adolescent (infantile?) rage. This is not the polished work of Hemingway or Faulkner as novelist or even as essayist, but the writing of men reacting informally—but intensely—to how they are perceived by one another.

men were undergoing personal problems, monetary and marital as well as professional. Hemingway's reputation had already begun to depend more on public performance than on literary merit, and the withered sales of Faulkner's work left his reputation buried in the academy, its worth apparent to a handful of professors and a few serious students of fiction. Once more, Malcolm Cowley's role was important. His *Viking Portable* editions, (*Hemingway* in 1944, *Faulkner* in 1946), each a critical anthology providing an admirable introduction to the men and their work, guaranteed them not mere revival but a substantial new and enthusiastic readership. Paradoxically, Cowley's efforts may have goaded each of them to utter careless but provocative statements certain to assure incendiary response. It was the reticent Faulkner who—in a university classroom—unwitting and wholly without malice, nevertheless ignited the fire, then fanned the flame.

In April, 1947, Faulkner had contracted with the University of Mississippi (for $250) to offer informal lectures and wide-ranging open discussions about literature. Although Faulkner's contract made clear that notes were not to be taken, they were, and some soon appeared in public print. Excerpts from one of those reports—five brief paragraphs based on notes taken by the director of public relations at the university, Marvin Black—appeared in the *Saturday Review* in April and, in May, in the *New York Herald-Tribune*'s book review section. When Faulkner learned that the public relations department of the University intended to release the material, he was furious. But when assured that the material would be distributed only locally and that the university administration wanted a return engagement of this overwhelmingly popular series, Faulkner accepted an apology and went on vacation.

What crimes had Faulkner committed? Two, the first, multi-pronged: ranking his fellow contemporary American novelists, and including himself (after initially refusing out of modesty). He ordered them so: Wolfe, Faulkner, Dos Passos, Hemingway, and Steinbeck. The basis for his judgment was, the reporter recalled, the degree by which each of them had failed to capture the range and significance of human experience. Each had failed, but to Faulkner, their ranking rested upon "the splendor of the failure."

Faulkner's second "crime" lay in indicting Hemingway as a "coward" (he used the word), a writer who "has no courage, has never climbed out on a limb. He has never used a word where the reader might check his usage by a dictionary." (Blotner, 1231–35). Bad enough that Faulkner listed himself above Hemingway, worse was that he challenged Hemingway's courage. Faulkner's timing could not have been worse since Hemingway was at this time by his own admission profoundly depressed, sulking at Finca Vigia in what he called a "black ass" mood. Rather than reply himself, Hemingway asked his wartime friend, General Buck Lanham, to set the record straight on courage, which Lanham did, calling Hemingway "the most courageous man I have ever known, both in war and peace." (cited in Baker, 461).

Appalled at the uproar his comments had caused, Faulkner apologized at once to both Lanham and Hemingway, denying that his comment bore "any reference whatever to Hemingway as a man: only to his craftsmanship as a writer." The courage Faulkner found wanting lay in Hemingway's failure to "risk bad taste, over-writing, dullness, etc." (Blotner, 1235). Some years later, he extended his reasons for dropping Hemingway below Wolfe and himself (in fact, he now placed Hemingway last) saying "within what he knew. He did it fine, but he didn't try for the impossible." Others, especially Wolfe, "had tried to do the greatest of the impossible . . . to reduce all human experience to literature." (cited in Breit, 184).

Hemingway's letter responding to Faulkner (23 July 1947) resides in Boston in the JFK Library. Whether it was ever mailed remains uncertain:

Dear Bill:

Awfully glad to hear from you and glad to have made contact. Your letter came tonight and please throw all the other stuff away, the misunderstanding, or will have to come up and we both trompel [sic] on it. There isn't any at all. I was sore and Buck [Lanham] was sore and we were instantly unsore the minute we knew the score. . . .

You are a better writer than Fielding or any of those guys and you should just know it and keep on writing. You have things written that come back to me better than any of them and I am not dopy, really. You shouldn't read the shit about liveing [sic] writers. . . . Anyway I am your Bro. if you want one that writes and I'd like us to keep in touch. . . . Excuse chickenshit letter. Have much regard for you. Would like to keep on writing. Ernest Hemingway (Baker, *Selected Letters* 623–25).

The first serious confrontation—a rather silly set of misinterpretations about "courage"—ended in cautious cordiality, including Hemingway's telling a friend that he had cabled his congratulations to Faulkner upon winning the Nobel in 1949, adding that Faulkner was a nice guy and deserved the Prize.

The détente lasted until June, 1952 when once more Faulkner unintentionally provoked Hemingway's wrath. In a letter to Harvey Breit (20 June 1952), a features editor at the book review of the *New York Times*, Faulkner recalled once hearing Hemingway observe that "writers should stick together just as doctors and lawyers and wolves do." The image of the wolf pack, Faulkner continued, ill-suited a writer like Hemingway whose work made clear that he needed "no pack protection," that "the sort of writers who need to band together . . . resemble the wolves who are wolves only in pack, and singly, are just another dog." (Blotner, *Selected Letters*, 333–34). Certain that Hemingway would be pleased, Breit reported to him the content of

Faulkner's letter. Hemingway's response stunned Breit—a two-and-a half page explosion of rage and ramble. Why? Because Faulkner had called him a "dog." At worst, Faulkner's intended compliment was awkwardly phrased, but Hemingway's virulent *recitativo*, based on his failure of comprehension, is almost poignant in its portrait of a troubled mind. He begins by recalling how Faulkner had once apologized for calling him a coward. And now, "Me, the dog. I'll be a sad son of a bitch." Hemingway goes on to denounce Faulkner for failing to acknowledge the congratulatory cable he'd sent when Faulkner won the Nobel Prize, adding a sneering comment that "so long as I am alive he has to drink to feel good about haveing [*sic*] the Nobel Prize." He includes as well references to Faulkner's decline as a writer: ". . . he has the one great and un-curable defect; you can't re-read him." In a pitiable postscript he admits that although he's been too hard on Faulkner, ". . . I know I am not as hard on him as I am on myself." He begs Breit not to tell Faulkner any of what he has written: "I do not want any quarrels."(*Letters*, 769–73).

Faulkner never learned about Hemingway's broadside, its mockery of the Mississipian's syntax, his crabbed county, Anomatopeoio (Yoknapatawpha), or his inability to learn how to finish a book.

Unaware of Hemingway's outburst, Faulkner had just read *The Old Man and the Sea* and cabled Hemingway: "Splendid news. Stop not that quote the old man unquote needs more accolade than it already has from us who know the anguish it took and have tried to do it too. Bill Faulkner." (Blotner, *Selected Letters*, 348). Moreover, in a brief but enthusiastic review of the novel for a little magazine, Faulkner wrote: "His best. Time may show it to be the best single piece of any of us, I mean his and my contemporaries. . . ."

What Faulkner added, however, disgruntled Hemingway more than the praise pleased. Hemingway, he went on, had at last "discovered God, a Creator. Until now, his men and women had made themselves, shaped themselves out of their own clay; their victories and defeats were at the hands of each other, just to prove to themselves or one another how tough they could be. But this time, he wrote about pity; about something somewhere that made them all . . . made them all and loved them all and pitied them all. . . . It's all right. Praise God that whatever made and loves and pities Hemingway and me kept him from touching it any further. . . ." (*Shenandoah*, 1952. Cited in Blotner, 1428–29). Such abstraction may well have sickened Hemingway. In a letter to Charles Poore written soon afterward, Hemingway complained : ". . . when Bill Faulkner talks about God as though he knew him intimately and had the word I would have to answer that I do not know." (Bruccoli, *Hemingway at Auction*, 168; see also Flannery O'Connor's response to Faulkner's review, above, p.114).

During the few years remaining to them, Hemingway and Faulkner kept scratching the same sores. Once Faulkner had won the Nobel, Hemingway wrote to friends that Faulkner lacked moral fiber, adding the gratuitous information that he was as much of a prick as Edgar Allan Poe. Turning to other pieces of Faulkner's fiction, Hemingway wrote: "Some of Faulkner's 'Southern stuff' and 'some of the Negro stuff' was very good, including 'The Bear.' His most readable work was *Sanctuary* and *Pylon. A Fable*, however, was not pure shit but 'impure diluted shit,' and the man himself was a no-good son of a bitch." (Letter to Mr. Rider, July 29,1956. *Hemingway at Auction*, 83).

Faulkner, back in the classroom at the University of Virginia, also continued to revisit the past. Invited once more in 1958 to talk about the "rankings controversy," Faulkner said: "I meant only that Hemingway had sense enough to find a method which he could control and didn't need or didn't have to, wasn't driven by his private demon to waste himself trying to do more than that. So, he has done consistently probably the most solid work of all of us. But it wasn't the splendid magnificent bust that Wolfe made in trying to put the whole history of the human heart on the head of the pin. . . ." (*Faulkner in the University*, 143–44).

When the subject shifted from rankings to readings however, Faulkner's demeanor relaxed. No longer defensive (and certainly not aggressive), he addressed issues and works with clarity and repect. Had he ever put himself in a story as Hemingway had? "No," he answered, "and I don't think Hemingway does it either. I think that any writer worth his salt is convinced that he can create much better people than God can. . . ." (*Faulkner in the University*, 118). When queried about specific novels, however, he raised the level of discussion beyond where Hemingway had abandoned both taste and decorum. Asked, for example, whether *For Whom the Bell Tolls* was "didactic," Faulkner replied that Hemingway "was writing the story . . . which seemed to him moving and tragic, which like all writers he never told well enough to please him . . . he was not really writing primarily about the Spanish Civil War, but he was writing about the human condition which to him was moving and tragic. . . ." (*Faulkner in the University*, 182–83).

When Truman Capote trashed *Across the River*, Faulkner chided him: "Young man," he said, "I haven't read this new one. And though it may not be the best thing Hemingway ever wrote, I know it will be carefully done, and it will have quality." (Blotner, 1308). When critical rejections of *Across the River* continued—so did Faulkner continue to reject the rejections. Hemingway needed no defense, he argued, because "the ones who didn't write *Men Without Women* and *The Sun Also Rises* and the African pieces and the rest of it don't have anything to stand on while they throw the spitballs." (Blotner, 1334)

Finally, soon after Hemingway's suicide, and just a year before his own death, Faulkner's grim response to the event starkly illuminates the huge difference between their attitudes toward the sanctity of family and extramarital dalliance: "It's bad when a man does something like that. It's like saying, death is better than living with my wife. . . ."(Blotner, 179). One wonders how Hemingway would have reacted to Faulkner's daring to judge how he died.

With all their saying said, their voices stopped. The two dominant figures in American fiction from the 1920s through the 1950s died within a year of one another, Hemingway just short of his sixty-second birthday in July, 1961, Faulkner a year later at sixty-five. Their final years were beset with pain. Hemingway's body had been ravaged by a lifetime of injuries, excessive drinking, high blood pressure and diabetes, as well as a dangerous inherited ailment (hemachromatosis), Faulkner's by a long history of alcoholism (he was regularly sent away to dry out) and, at the last, by heavy dosages of drugs and alcohol to ease the back pain caused by a fall from his horse. Rumors that Faulkner chose to end his life by what he knew would be a final and fatal binge were vigorously denied by those closest to him. The official announcement was that he died quietly of a coronary occlusion. Hemingway's death was louder and, like the man, more dramatic.

Beyond the agonies of their bodies was the perhaps more intolerable mental torment they suffered. Both were plagued by diminished memory, flagging imagination, and frequent and profound depressions, for which each had undergone shock therapy. True, Hemingway worked till the end (see the posthumously published *A Moveable Feast* and *True at First Light*) but he was unable to complete any of these texts. His despair and anxiety led to delusion (he was convinced the IRS was after him), electroshock therapy, and several failed attempts at suicide until the last successful one—a double-barreled shotgun angled against his hard palate and discharged.

What impact Hemingway's death had upon Faulkner (see his letter above) cannot be definitely assessed. But, as Frederick Karl observes,

"The two were intertwined . . . Faulkner saw in the other's death some-thing of his own. It was not only the death of Hemingway, however, but the end of an era in American writing: the few great ones had passed. Faulkner felt there was no one to replace them." (Karl, 1037)

In his lyric portrait of Crispin in "The Comedian as the Letter C," Wallace Stevens captured something of the legacy both Hemingway and Faulkner contributed to American letters:

> He gripped more closely the essential prose
> As being, in a world so falsified,
> To which all poems were incident, unless
> That prose should wear a poem's guise at last.

Or, if we may risk a sentimentality that both writers would almost certainly decry, the larks, still bravely singing, fly.

BIBLIOGRAPHICAL MATERIALS

During the late 1930s and throughout the 1940s, the reputations of Hemingway and Faulkner gradually—and naturally—shifted from the hands and minds of their fellow writers to become the responsibility of the critics and, eventually, the Academy. The process was complex, the causes many: the emergence of prestigious literary journals, some independent (*Partisan Review*), others with academic affiliation (*Kenyon Review, Sewanee Review, The Southern Review*); the increasing dominance of the New Criticism in English departments; the post–WWII explosion in college enrollments and a concomitant modernization of syllabi; and the emergence of a new generation of fiction writers and poets acutely aware of their debt to Hemingway and Faulkner. We have appended a short list of articles representing this transition to a more professional system of interpretation and evaluation.

A Short List of Articles Representative of the Transition to Professional Interpretation and Evaluation

About Hemingway:

Schwartz, Delmore. "Ernest Hemingway's Literary Situation." *Southern Review* 3 (1938): 769–82.

Trilling, Lionel. "Hemingway and His Critics." *Partisan Review* 6 (Winter 1939): 52–60.

Wilson, Edmund. "Hemingway: Bourdon Gauge of Morale." *The Atlantic Monthly* 164 (July 1939): 36–46. Reprinted in *The Wound and the Bow: Seven Studies in Literature*. Boston: Houghton Mifflin, 1941, 214–42.

Warren, Robert Penn. "Ernest Hemingway," *Kenyon Review* 9 (Winter 1947): 1–28.
Cowley, Malcolm. "A Portrait of Mister Papa." *Life* 25 (Jan.10, 1949): 86–101.

About Faulkner:

O'Donnell, George Marion. "Faulkner's Mythology." *Kenyon Review* 1 (Summer 1939): 285–99.
Beck, Warren. "Faulkner and the South." *Antioch Review* 1 (March 1941): 82–94.
———. "Faulkner's Point of View." *College English* 2 (May 1941): 736–49.
Schwartz, Delmore. "The Fiction of William Faulkner." *Southern Review* 7 (Summer 1941): 145–60.
Cowley, Malcolm. "Introduction," *The Portable Faulkner* (New York: Viking), 1946.

A Select List of Works

Aiken, Conrad
Senlin: A Biography, and Other Poems, 1918
Blue Voyage, 1927
Ushant, 1952

Algren, Nelson
The Man with the Golden Arm, 1956
A Walk on the Wild Side, 1956

Anderson, Sherwood
Winesburg, Ohio, 1919
The Triumph of the Egg, 1921
Horses and Men, 1923
A Story Teller's Story, 1924

Auden W(ystan) H(ugh)
The Dog Beneath the Skin, 1935

The Age of Anxiety, 1947
The Shield of Achilles, 1955

Basso, Hamilton
Cinnamon Seed, 1934
Sun in Capricorn, 1942
The View from Pompey's Head, 1954

Beach, Sylvia
Shakespeare & Company, 1958

Bishop, Elizabeth
North and South, 1946
The Complete Poems, 1970

Bishop, John Peale
Many Thousands Gone, 1931

Collected Poems, 1948
Act of Darkness, 1935

Bogan, Louise
Body of This Death, 1923
Dark Summer, 1929
The Sleeping Fury, 1937

Boyle, Kay
Nothing Ever Breaks the Heart, 1966
Collected Poems, 1991

Brooks, Cleanth (with Robert Penn
    Warren)
Understanding Poetry, 1938
Understanding Fiction, 1943

Burke, Kenneth
The Philosophy of Literary Form,
    1941
A Grammar of Motives, 1945
A Rhetoric of Motives, 1950

Caldwell, Erskine
Tobacco Road, 1932
God's Little Acre, 1933
You Have Seen Their Faces, 1937
    (with Margaret Bourke-White)

Capote, Truman
Other Voices, Other Rooms, 1948
Breakfast at Tiffany's, 1958
In Cold Blood, 1966

Cowley, Malcolm
Blue Juniata, 1929
Exile's Return: A Narrative of Ideas,
    1934

Crane, Hart
White Buildings, 1926
The Bridge, 1930

Crosby, Harry
Shadows of the Sun, 1928
Transit of Venus, 1928
War Letters, 1932

Cummings, E. E.
The Enormous Room, 1922
Tulips and Chimneys, 1923
Eimi, 1933
Collected Poems, 1938

Davidson, Donald
The Piper, 1924

Doolittle, Hilda [H.D.]
Hymen, 1921
Heliodora and Other Poems, 1924
Tribute to Freud, 1956
Bid Me to Live, 1960

Dos Passos, John
Three Soldiers, 1921
Manhattan Transfer, 1925
U.S.A. 1930, 1932, 1936

Ellison, Ralph
Invisible Man, 1952
Flying Home and Other Stories, 1997
Juneteenth, 1999

Farrell, James T.
The Lonigan Trilogy, 1932, 1934,
    1935
A World I Never Made, 1936

Fitzgerald, F. Scott
This Side of Paradise, 1920
The Beautiful and Damned, 1922
The Great Gatsby, 1925
Tender is the Night, 1934

Frost, Robert
A Boy's Will, 1913
North of Boston, 1914
New Hampshire, 1923
Collected Poems, 1939

Gordon, Caroline
Penhally, 1931
Aleck Maury, Sportsman, 1934
The Malefactors, 1956

Guthrie, Ramon
Asbestos Phoenix, 1969
Maximum Security Ward, 1970

Hammett, Dashiell
Red Harvest, 1929
The Maltese Falcon, 1930
The Thin Man, 1932

Herbst, Josephine
Nothing Is Sacred, 1928
The Starched Blue Sky of Spain, 1991

Lewis, Sinclair
Main Street, 1920
Babbitt, 1922
Arrowsmith, 1925
Elmer Gantry, 1927

MacLeish, Archibald
The Hamlet of A. MacLeish, 1928

Conquistador, 1932
J.B., 1958

McAlmon, Robert
The Portrait of a Generation, 1926
Being Geniuses Together, 1938

Mencken, H. L.
Prejudices, 1919–1927
The American Language, 1918–1948

Miller, Henry
Tropic of Cancer, 1934
Tropic of Capricorn, 1939
The Rosy Crucifixion trilogy
   (1949–60)

Moore, Marianne
Observations, 1924
Collected Poems, 1951
Complete Poems, 1967

Morris, Wright
The Field of Vision, 1956
Will's Boy, 1981

O'Connor, Flannery
A Good Man is Hard to Find, 1955
The Violent Bear it Away, 1960
*Everything that Rises Must Con-
   verge*, 1965

O'Hara, John
Appointment in Samarra, 1934
Butterfield 8, 1935
A Rage to Live, 1949

Porter, Katherine Anne
Flowering Judas, 1930

Pale Horse, Pale Rider, 1939
The Leaning Tower, 1944
Ship of Fools, 1962

Pound, Ezra
Personae, 1909
Hugh Selwyn Mauberly, 1920
Cantos, 1919–1970
ABC of Reading, 1934

Powell, Dawn
Dance Night, 1930
A Time To Be Born, 1942

Ransom, John Crowe
Chills and Fever, 1924
God Without Thunder, 1930
The World's Body, 1938
Selected Poems, 1945

Roethke, Theodore
Collected Poems, 1966

Sandburg, Carl
Chicago Poems, 1916
Smoke and Steel, 1920
Good Morning, America, 1928
Complete Poems, 1950

Saroyan, William
The Daring Young Man on the Flying Trapeze, 1934
The Time of Your Life, 1939
My Name is Aram, 1940

Schneider, Isidor
Dr. Transit, 1925
Temptation of Anthony, 1927
Kingdom of Necessity, 1935

Schwartz, Delmore
In Dreams Begin Responsibilities, 1938
The World Is a Wedding, 1948

Evelyn Scott
Escapades, 1923
The Wave, 1929

Stein, Gertrude
Three Lives, 1909
Tender Buttons, 1914
The Making of Americans, 1925
The Autobiography of Alice B. Toklas, 1933

Steinbeck, John
The Pastures of Heaven, 1932
In Dubious Battle, 1936
Of Mice and Men, 1937
The Grapes of Wrath, 1939

Stevens, Wallace
Harmonium, 1923
The Man with the Blue Guitar, 1937
Collected Poems, 1954

Tate, Allen
Mr. Pope and Other Poems, 1928
Reactionary Essays on Poetry and Ideas, 1938
Poems, 1922–1947, 1948

Teasdale, Sara
Love Songs, 1917
Collected Poems, 1937

Thurber, James
Is Sex Necesssary (with E. B. White), 1929

The Middle-Aged Man on the Flying Trapeze, 1935
The Thurber Carnival, 1945

Warren, Robert Penn
Selected Poems, 1923–43, 1944
All the King's Men, 1946
Circus in the Attic, 1948
World Enough and Time, 1950

Wharton, Edith
The House of Mirth, 1905
Ethan Frome, 1911
The Custom of the Country, 1913
The Age of Innocence, 1920

Welty, Eudora
Delta Wedding, 1946
The Golden Apples, 1949
The Ponder Heart, 1954

Wescott, Glenway
The Grandmothers, 1927
Pilgrim Hawk, 1940
Apartment in Athens, 1945

White, E. B.
Stuart Little, 1945
Charlotte's Web, 1952

Wilder, Thornton
The Bridge of San Luis Rey, 1927

Our Town, 1938
The Skin of Our Teeth, 1948

Williams, Tennessee
The Glass Menagerie, 1945
A Streetcar Named Desire, 1947
Cat on a Hot Tin Roof, 1955

Williams, William Carlos
Kora in Hell, 1920
In the American Grain, 1925
White Mule, 1937
Paterson, 1946–58

Wilson, Edmund
I Thought of Daisy, 1929
Axel's Castle, 1931
To the Finland Station, 1940
The Wound and the Bow, 1941
Memoirs of Hecate County, 1946

Wolfe, Thomas
Look Homeward, Angel, 1929
Of Time and the River, 1935
The Web and the Rock, 1939
You Can't Go Home Again, 1940

Wright, Richard
Native Son, 1940
Black Boy, 1945
White Man, Listen, 1957

Young, Stark
So Red the Rose, 1934

A Short List of the Writings of Ernest Hemingway and William Faulkner

Hemingway:

The Sun Also Rises, 1925
A Farewell to Arms, 1929
Death in the Afternoon, 1931
The Fifth Column and the First Forty-Nine Stories, 1938
For Whom the Bell Tolls, 1940
The Old Man and the Sea, 1952

Posthumous Work:
A Moveable Feast, 1964
Islands in the Stream, 1970
Garden of Eden, 1986
Complete Short Stories, 1987
True at First Light, 1999

Faulkner:

The Sound and the Fury, 1929
As I Lay Dying, 1930
Sanctuary, 1931
Light in August, 1932
Absalom, Absalom! 1936
Go Down, Moses, 1942
Collected Short Stories, 1950
A Fable, 1954
The Reivers, 1962

WORKS CITED

n.a. *We Moderns: 1920–1940,* Catalogue No. 42. New York: Gotham Book Mart, 1940.

Aaron, Daniel. *Writers on the Left.* New York: Harcourt Brace & World, 1961.

Arnold, Edwin T., ed. *Conversations with Erskine Caldwell,* Jackson: U of Mississippi P, 1988.

Baker, Carlos. *Ernest Hemingway: A Life Story.* New York: Scribner's, 1969.

———. ed. *Ernest Hemingway: Selected Letters, 1917–1961.* New York: Scribner's, 1981.

Basmadjian, Garig. "Candid Conversation," in *William Saroyan: The Man and the Writer Remembered,* ed. Leo Hamalian. New Jersey: Fairleigh Dickinson UP, 1987.

Bayley, Isabel, ed. *Letters of Katherine Anne Porter.* New York: Atlantic Monthly Press, 1990.

Beach, Sylvia. *Shakespeare and Company.* London: Faber, 1959.

Benson, Jackson J. *The True Adventures of John Steinbeck, Writer.* New York: Viking, 1984.

Blotner, Joseph. *Faulkner: A Biography.* 2 vols. New York: Random House, 1974.

———. ed. *Selected Letters of William Faulkner.* New York: Random House, 1977.

Bode, Carl, ed. *The New Mencken Letters.* New York: Dial Press, 1977.

Boyd, Brian. *Vladimir Nabokov: The American Years.* Princeton, NJ: Princeton UP, 1994.

Brazeau, Peter. *Parts of a World: Wallace Stevens Remembered.* New York: Random House, 1977.

Breit, Harvey. *The Writer Observed*. New York: Collier Books, 1961.

Brenner, Gerry. *A Comprehensive Companion to Hemingway's "A Moveable Feast."* Lewiston, NY: The Edwin Mellen Press, 2000.

Bruccoli, Matthew J. *Scott and Ernest: The Fitzgerald Hemingway Friendship*. New York: Random House, 1978.

———. *Some Sort of Epic Grandeur: The Life of F. Scott Fitzgerald*. New York: Harcourt Brace Jovanovich, 1981.

———. *The Only Thing That Counts:The Ernest Hemingway–Maxwell Perkins Correspondence:1925–1947*. U of South Carolina P, 1996.

Bruccoli, Matthew J. and C. E. Frazer Clark, Jr., eds. *Hemingway at Auction: 1930–1973*. Detroit: A Bruccoli–Clark Book, Gale Research, 1973; U of South Carolina P, 1999.

Burns, Edward, ed. *Letters of Alice B. Toklas: Staying on Alone*. New York: Vintage Books, 1975.

Campbell, Hilbert H., ed. *The Sherwood Anderson Diaries:1936–1941*. Athens: U of Georgia P, 1987.

Collins, Carvel, ed. *William Faulkner: Early Prose and Poetry*. Boston: Little, Brown and Company, 1962.

Cowley, Malcolm. *The Faulkner–Cowley File: Letters and Memories, 1944–1962*. New York: The Viking Press (Compass Edition), 1968.

Dardis, Tom. *Some Time in the Sun*. New York: Charles Scribner's Sons, 1976.

———. *Firebrand: The Life of Horace Liveright*. New York: Random House, 1995.

Davenport-Hines, Richard. *Auden*. NY: Pantheon Books, 1995.

Davidson, Donald. *The Attack on Leviathan*. Chapel Hill: U of North Carolina P, 1938.

Donahue, H. E. F. *Conversations with Nelson Algren*. New York: Hill & Wang, 1964.

Donaldson, Scott. *Fool for Love*. New York: Congdon and Weed, 1983.

———. *Hemingway vs. Fitzgerald: The Rise and Fall of a Literary Friendship*. Woodstock, NY: The Overlook Press, 1999.

Dos Passos, John. *The Best Time: An Informal Memoir*. New York: New American Library,1966.

———. *The Fourteenth Chronicle: Letters and Diaries of John Dos Passos*, ed. Townsend Ludington. Boston: Gambit, 1973.

Drake, William. *Sara Teasdale: A Woman & Poet*. San Francisco: Harper & Row, 1979.

Drew, Bettina. *Nelson Algren: A Life on the Wild Side*. New York: G. P. Putnam's Sons, 1989.

Dupee, F. W. and George Stade, eds. *Selected Letters of E. E. Cummings*. New York: Harcourt Brace & World, 1969.

Eby, Carl P. *Hemingway's Fetishism: Psychoanalysis and the Mirror of Manhood*. New York: State U of Albany P, 1998.

Elias, Robert H., ed. *Letters of Theodore Dreiser*. Philadelphia: U of Pennsylvania P, 1959.

Eliot, T. S. "Commentary." *The Criterion* (XII, 1933) 466–73.

Fain, John T. and Thomas D. Young, eds. *The Literary Correspondence of Donald Davidson and Allen Tate*. Athens: U Georgia P, 1974.

Fitch, Noel Riley. *Sylvia Beach and The Lost Generation: A History of Literary Paris in the Twenties and Thirties*. New York: W. W. Norton, 1983.

Fiedler, Leslie. "The Ant and the Grasshopper," (review of Frederick J. Hoffman's *The Twenties: American Writing in the Post-War Decade*), *Partisan Review* (Summer, 1955) 412–17.

Fitzgerald, Sally, ed. *The Habit of Being: Letters of Flannery O'Connor*. New York: Farrar, Straus & Giroux, 1979.

Ford, Hugh. *Published in Paris*. New York: Macmillan, 1975.

Gall, Sally, ed. *Ramon Guthrie: Maximum Security Ward and Other Poems*. New York: Persea Press, 1984.

Gelderman, Carol, ed. *Conversations with Mary McCarthy*. Jackson: U of Mississippi P, 1991.

Gerber, Philip L. and Joan Rubin [Interviewers]. "Day of Doom, Day of Dreams: Malcolm Cowley on the 1930s," *Horns of Plenty*, 2:2 (Summer, 1989) 36–51.

Gerogiannis, Nicholas, ed. *Ernest Hemingway: 88 Poems*. New York: Harcourt Brace Jovanovich, 1979.

Giroux, Robert, ed. *One Art: Letters Selected and Edited*. New York: Farrar, Straus & Giroux, 1994.

Grobel, Lawrence. *Conversations with Capote*. New York: NAL, 1985.

Gwynn, Frederick L. and Joseph L. Blotner, eds. *Faulkner in the University*. New York: Vintage, 1965.

Guest, Barbara. *Herself Defined: The Poet H.D. and Her World*. New York: Doubleday, 1984.

Guth, Dorothy Lobrano, ed. *Letters of E. B. White*, New York: Harper & Row, 1976.

Hammer, Langdon and Brom Weber, eds. *O My Land, My Friends: The Selected Letters of Hart Crane*. New York: Four Walls, Eight Windows, 1997.

Hanneman, Audre. *Ernest Hemingway: A Comprehensive Biography*. Princeton: Princeton U Press, 1967.

Hemingway, Ernest. *A Moveable Feast*. New York: Scribner's, 1964.

———. *True at First Light*. Ed. Patrick Hemingway. New York: Scribner's, 1999.

Herbst, Josephine. *The Starched Blue Sky of Spain and Other Memoirs*. New York: HarperCollins, 1991.

Jay, Paul, ed. *The Selected Correspondence of Kenneth Burke and Malcolm Cowley: 1915–1981*. Berkeley: U of California P, 1990.

Jones, Howard Mumford and Walter Rideout, eds. *The Letters of Sherwood Anderson*. Boston: Little Brown, 1953.

Karl, Frederick R. *William Faulkner: American Writer*. New York: Weidenfeld & Nicholson, 1989.

Keisnowski, Frank and Alice Hughes, eds. *Conversations with Henry Miller*. Jackson: UP of Mississippi, 1944.

Kinney, Harrison with Rosemary A. Thurber, eds. *The Thurber Letters*. NY: Simon & Schuster, 2002.

Krystal, Arthur, ed. *A Company of Readers: Uncollected Writings of Auden, Barzun, and Trilling*. New York: Free Press, 1991.

Layman, Richard with Julie M. Rivett, eds. *Selected Letters of Dashiell Hammett*. Washington, D.C.: Counterpoint, 2001.

Lee, Hermione. "The Unknown Edith Wharton," (book review), *The New York Review of Books*, October 4, 2001.

Lewis, Wyndham. *Men Without Art*. Ed. Seamus Cooney. Santa Rosa: Black Sparrow Press, 1934; revised and corrected, 1987.

Lindberg-Seynsted, Brita, ed., *Pound/Ford: The Story of a Literary Friendship*, New York: New Directions, 1982.

Limmer, Ruth, ed. *What the Woman Lived: Selected Letters of Louise Bogan: 1920–1970*. New York: Harcourt Brace Jovanovich, 1973.

Litwak, Leo. "Kay Boyle—Paris Wasn't Like That," (an interview) *The New York Times Book Review,* July 15, 1984.

MacShane, Frank. *The Life of John O'Hara.* New York: Dutton, 1980.

Mariani, Paul. *William Carlos Williams: A New World Naked.* New York: McGraw Hill, 1981.

Millgate, Michael. *The Achievement of William Faulkner.* New York: Random House, 1966.

McAlmon, Robert. *Being Geniuses Together 1920–30 (Revised and with supplementary chapters by Kay Boyle).* New York: Doubleday & Co., 1968.

McCarthy, Mary. *Intellectual Memoirs: 1936–1938.* New York, Harcourt, Brace, Jovanovich, 1992.

Meade, Marion. *Dorothy Parker: What Fresh Hell Is This?* New York: Villard Books, 1988.

Mellen, Joan. *Hellmann and Hammett: The Legendary Passion of Lillian Hellmann and Dashiell Hammett.* New York: HarperCollins, 1996.

Mellow, James R. *Charmed Circle: Gertrude Stein and Company.* New York: Praeger Publishers, 1974.

Meyers, Jeffrey. *Hemingway: A Biography.* New York: Harper & Row, 1985.

Mitgang, Herbert, ed. *The Letters of Carl Sandburg.* New York: Harcourt Brace & World, 1968.

Morris, Wright. *About Fiction: Reverent Reflections on the Nature of Fiction with Irreverent Observations on Writers, Readers, and Other Abuses.* New York: Harper & Row, 1975.

Murray, Albert and John F. Callahan, eds. *Trading Twelves: The Selected Letters of Ralph Ellison and Albert Murray.* New York: Vintage Books, 2001.

Nowell, Elizabeth, ed. *The Letters of Thomas Wolfe.* New York: Scribner's, 1956.

Page, Tim, ed. *The Diaries of Dawn Powell: 1931–1965.* Vermont: Steerforth Press, 1995.

———. *Selected Letters of Dawn Powell: 1913–1965.* New York: Henry Holt & Co., 1999.

Paige, D. D., ed. *The Letters of Ezra Pound: 1907–41.* New York: Harcourt Brace, 1950.

Parker, Dorothy. "The Artist's Reward," a "Profile" in *The New Yorker,* (November 30, 1929) 23–29.

Phillips, Robert, ed. *Letters of Delmore Schwartz*. Princeton: Ontario Review Press, 1984.

Pilkington, John, ed. *Stark Young: A Life in the Arts, Letters, 1900–1962*. Baton Rouge: Louisiana State UP, 1975.

Plimpton, George, ed. "Robert Penn Warren," *Writers at Work: First Series*. New York: Viking, 1958.

———. "James Thurber," *Writers at Work: First Series*. New York: Viking, 1958.

———. "Ernest Hemingway," *Writers at Work: Second Series*. New York: Viking, 1963.

———. "Ralph Ellison," *Writers at Work: Second Series*. New York: Viking, 1963.

———. "John Dos Passos," *Writers at Work: Fourth Series*. New York: Viking, 1976.

———. "Eudora Welty," *Writers at Work: Fourth Series*. New York: Viking, 1976.

———. "Archibald MacLeish," *Writers at Work: Fifth Series*. New York: Viking, 1981.

Reynolds, Michael. *Hemingway: The Paris Years*. Oxford: Basil Blackwell Ltd., 1989. New York: W. W. Norton, Inc., 1999.

———. *Hemingway: The 1930s*. New York: W. W. Norton, Inc., 1997.

Richardson, Joan. *Wallace Stevens: A Biography: The Later Years*. New York: William Morrow, 1988.

Robbins, Jack Alan, ed. *James T. Farrell: Literary Essays*. Port Washington: Kennikat Press, 1976.

Rock, Virginia. "Dualisms in Agrarian Thought," *The Mississippi Quarterly* (Spring, 1960) 80–89.

Ross, Lillian. "How Do You Like It Now, Gentlemen?" *The New Yorker*, (May 13, 1950) 36–62.

———. *Portrait of Hemingway*. New York: Simon & Schuster, 1961.

———. *Portrait of Hemingway* (with a new Afterword by the author). NY: Modern Library, 1997.

———. *Reporting Back; Notes on Journalism*. New York: Counterpoint, 2002.

Schorer, Mark. *Sinclair Lewis: An American Life*. New York: McGraw-Hill, 1961.

Sheaffer, Louis. *O'Neill: Son and Artist.* Boston: Little, Brown and Company, 1973.

Simpson, Louis. *Three on the Tower: The Lives and Works of Ezra Pound, T. S. Eliot and William Carlos Williams.* New York: William Morrow, 1975.

Steinbeck, Elaine and Robert Wallston, eds. *Steinbeck: A Life in Letters.* New York: Viking, 1975.

Stevens, Holly, ed. *Letters of Wallace Stevens.* New York: Knopf, 1966.

Stevens, Wallace. *Collected Poems.* New York: Knopf, 1955.

Stuhlmann, Gunther, eds. *Henry Miller: Letters to Anais Nin.* New York: G. P. Putnam's Sons, 1965.

Svoboda, Frederic J. *Hemingway & The Sun Also Rises: The Crafting of a Style.* Lawrence: U of Kansas P, 1983.

Thompson, James, Lennox Raphael and Steve Cannon, (interviewers). "A Very Stern Discipline: An Interview with Ralph Ellison," *Harper's Magazine* (March, 1967) 76–95.

Thompson, Lawrance. *Robert Frost: The Years of Triumph.* New York: Holt, Rinehart, Winston, 1970.

Thompson, Lawrance and R. H. Winnick. *Robert Frost: The Later Years.* New York: Holt, Rinehart, Winston, 1976.

Townsend, Kim. *Sherwood Anderson.* Boston: Houghton Mifflin Company, 1987.

Turnbull, Andrew, ed. *The Letters of F. Scott Fitzgerald.* New York: Scribner, 1963; Dell, 1965.

———. *Thomas Wolfe: A Biography.* New York: Charles Scribner's Sons, 1970.

Van Vechten, Carl, ed. *Selected Writings of Gertrude Stein.* New York: Random House, 1946.

Vinh, Alphonse, ed. *Cleanth Brooks and Allen Tate: Collected Letters.* Missouri: U of Missouri P, 1998.

Waldron, Ann. *Close Connections: Caroline Gordon and the Southern Renaissance.* New York: Putnam, 1987.

Wescott, Glenway. "Foreword" to Hugh Ford, *Four Lives in Paris.* San Francisco: North Point Press, 1987.

Walker, Margaret. *Richard Wright: Daemonic Genius.* New York: Warner Books, 1988.

Wilde, Meta Carpenter and Orin Borsten. *A Loving Gentleman: The Love Story of William Faulkner and Meta Carpenter*. New York: Simon & Schuster, 1976.

Wilder, Thornton. *The Journals of Thornton Wilder, 1939–1961*, selected and edited by Donald Gallup. New Haven: Yale UP, 1985.

Williams, Tennessee. *Memoirs*. New York: Doubleday & Co., 1975.

Wilson, Elena, ed. *Edmund Wilson: Letters on Literature and Politics: 1912–1972*. New York: Farrar Straus & Giroux, 1977.

Winnick, R. H., ed. *Letters of Archibald MacLeish*. Boston: Houghton Mifflin, 1983.

Wolff, Geoffrey. *Black Sun: The Brief Transit and Violent Eclipse of Harry Crosby*. New York: Random House, 1976.

Young, Thomas Daniel and John J. Hindle, eds. *The Republic of Letters in America: The Correspondence of John Peale Bishop & Allen Tate*. Lexington: UP of Kentucky, 1981.

Young, Thomas D. and George Core, eds. *Selected Letters of John Crowe Ransom*. Baton Rouge: U of Louisiana P, 1985.

ACKNOWLEDGMENTS

AS STUDENTS AND teachers of American literature for close to five decades, we are especially aware of our good fortune in being part of an extraordinary group of people—our fellow students and scholars. To masters like Daniel Aaron, Gay Wilson Allen, Roger Asselineau, Oscar Cargill, Frederick Ives Carpenter, Richard Chase, Hennig Cohen, Leslie A. Fiedler, Frederick J. Hoffman, R. W. B. Lewis, Henry Nash Smith, Edward C. Wagenknecht, Philip Young; to our fellow members of the English Department at the City College of New York; to our friends in the Hemingway Society, especially the late Michael Reynolds and Paul Smith; and to all who have labored to place another shard in the mosaic of our collective understanding, we are deeply grateful. The word "colleague" may stem indirectly from the Latin, "to read together." For some fifty years—even alone in the classroom or at our desks—we have been privileged to read in the company of dedicated, passionate, sometimes brilliant, unselfish colleagues.

And, most appropriately in this effort, we are humbled by the truth in the final couplet of Robert Frost's "The Tuft of Flowers":

"Men work together," I told him from the heart, / "Whether they work together or apart."

We acknowledge help and encouragement from interested and accommodating colleagues and friends, among them, sadly, the late Leo Hamalian and Frederick Karl; Susan Beegel, Lazare Bitoun, Gerry Brenner, Jackson Bryer, Jonathan and Jessica Crewe, William Herman, Leonard Kriegel, Ilse DuSoir Lind, Karl Malkoff, Alan Margolies, Janet Moore, Ruth Prigozy, Edward Quinn, Anne Saidman, Emily Schneider Schachter, Edmond Volpe, and Melissa Zeiger. We acknowledge with pleasure our children and their children. And finally, we acknowledge Evander Lomke who, years ago as a student at The City College of New York, skillfully avoided our classes, but as our editor has nonetheless acquired the craft, wit, and patience needed to guide us and our work to the fulfillment of publication.

Our particular thanks as well to those who have granted permission to reproduce the materials that are the spine and spirit of our work. In particular, our gratitude goes to Charles Scribner III whose generosity helped us from the start.

Excerpt from *True at First Light*, ed. Patrick Hemingway. Copyright © 1999. Charles Scribner's Sons. By permission of the publisher.

Excerpts from *Letters of Thomas Wolfe*, ed. Elizabeth Nowell. Copyright © 1956. Charles Scribner's Sons. By permission of the publisher.

Excerpts from *The Letters of F. Scott Fitzgerald*, ed. Andrew Turnbull. Copyright © 1963. Charles Scribner's Sons. By permission of the publisher.

Excerpts from unpublished letters of Isidor Schneider to Ernest Hemingway (1926–1927). Incoming Correspondence: Ernest Hemingway Collection at the John F. Kennedy Library, Boston, MA. With the permission of Emily Schneider Schachter.

Excerpts from Kim Townsend, *Sherwood Anderson*, Copyright © 1966. Boston: Houghton Mifflin Company. By permission of the author.

Excerpt from *The Letters of Sherwood Anderson*, eds. Howard Mumford Jones and Walter Rideout. Little, Brown, 1953. By permission of the Estate of Howard Mumford Jones and Eleanor Copenhaver Anderson Associates, c/o Harold Ober Associates.

An excerpt from *Ernest Hemingway: A Comprehensive Bibliography* by Audre Hannemann. Copyright © 1967, by permission of Princeton University Press.

Excerpts from *William Faulkner: American Writer* by Frederick R. Karl. New York: Weidenfeld & Nicolson, 1989, with the permission of the Estate of Frederick R. Karl.

Reprinted with permission of the University of Virginia Press from *Faulkner in the University*, Frederick Gwynn and Joseph Blotner, eds. (Charlottesville: Virginia, 1977, 1993).

Excerpts from John Dos Passos, *The Best Time: An Informal Memoir*. Copyright © 1966, New York: New American Library. By permission of Lucy Dos Passos Coggin.

Excerpted from *The Fourteenth Chronicle: Letters and Diaries of John Dos Passos*, edited by Townsend Ludington, Copyright © 1973, with permission from The Harvard Common Press, Boston, MA.

Excerpts from THE TRUE ADVENTURES OF JOHN STEIN-BECK, WRITER, by Jackson J. Benson, copyright © 1984 by Jackson J. Benson. Used by permission of Viking Penguin, a division of Penguin Group (USA) Inc.

"5/16/56 letter to James S. Pope" by John Steinbeck, from *STEIN-BECK: A LIFE IN LETTERS* by Elaine A. Steinbeck and Robert Wallsten, editors, copyright 1952, © 1969 by the Estate of John Steinbeck © 1975 by Elaine Steinbeck and Robert Wallsten. Used by permission of Viking Penguin, a division of Penguin Group (USA) Inc.

Excerpts from *CLOSE CONNECTIONS: CAROLINE GORDON AND THE SOUTHERN RENAISSANCE* by Ann Waldron, copyright © 1987. Used by permission of Putnam Penguin, a division of Penguin Group (USA) Inc.

"October 3,1929 to Cowley," "August 16, 1948, to Burke," by Malcolm Cowley, "February 22, 1963, to Cowley," from *SELECTED CORRESPONDENCE: 1915–1981* by Kenneth Burke and Malcolm Cowley, edited by Paul Jay, copyright © 1988 by Kenneth Burke, Malcolm Cowley, and Paul Jay. Used by permission of Viking Penguin, a division of Penguin Group (USA) Inc.

University of Nebraska Press for excerpts from Robert E. Knoll's *McAlmon and the Lost Generation.* Copyright © 1962.

Excerpts from Donald Gallup, ed. *The Journals of Thornton Wilder, 1939–1961*, copyright © 1985. By permission of Yale University Press.

Excerpts from *The Letters of Katherine Anne Porter*, ed. Isabel Bayley. Copyright © 1990. Atlantic Monthly Press. By permission of Grove/Atlantic.

Excerpts from Garig Basmadjian's "Candid Conversation," in *William Saroyan: The Man and the Writer Remembered*, ed. Leo Hamalian. New Jersey: Fairleigh Dickinson University Press, copyright © 1987. By permission of the editor and Fairleigh Dickinson University Press.

Excerpts from *The Letters of Archibald Macleish 1907–1982*, Edited by R. H. Winnick. Copyright © 1983 by The Estate of Archibald MacLeish and by R. H. Winnick. Reprinted by permission of Houghton Mifflin Company. All rights reserved.

Excerpts from *O My Land, My Friends: The Selected Letters of Hart Crane*, eds. Langdon Hammer and Brom Weber. Copyright © 1997, New York: Four Walls, Eight Windows. By permission of the publisher.

Excerpts from *Selected Letters of John Crowe Ransom*, eds. Thomas Daniel Young and George Core, copyright © 1985, Louisiana State University Press. Reprinted by permission of Louisiana State University Press.

Excerpts from Ramon Guthrie's "For Approximately the Same Reason Why a Man Can't Marry his Widow's Sister," collected in Gall, Sally, ed. *Ramon Guthrie: Maximum Security Ward and Other Poems*. New York: Persea Press, copyright © 1984. By permission of the Trustees of Dartmouth College.

Reprinted from *Cleanth Brooks and Allen Tate, 1933–1976* by Alphonse Vinh, by permission of the University of Missouri Press. Copyright © 1998 by the Curators of the University of Missouri and Helen Tate.

Excerpts from *Herself Defined: The Poet H.D. and her World* by Barbara Guest. New York: Doubleday, 1984 with the permission of the author.

From *LETTERS OF WALLACE STEVENS*, by Wallace Stevens, copyright © 1966 by Holly Stevens. Used by permission of Alfred A. Knopf, a division of Random House, Inc.

From *THE COLLECTED POEMS OF WALLACE STEVENS* by Wallace Stevens, copyright © 1954 by Wallace Stevens and renewed

1982 by Holly Stevens. Used by permission of Alfred A. Knopf, a division of Random House, Inc.

From *SELECTED LETTERS OF WILLIAM FAULKNER* by William Faulkner, edited by Joseph Blotner, copyright © 1977 by Jill Faulkner Summers. Used by permission of Random House, Inc.

From *FAULKNER: A BIOGRAPHY* by Joseph Blotner, copyright © 1974 by Joseph Blotner. Used by permission of Random House, Inc.

From *SELECTED WRITINGS OF GERTRUDE STEIN* by Gertrude Stein, edited by Carl Van Vechten, copyright © 1946 by Random House, Inc. Used by permission of Random House, Inc.

From *AUDEN* by Richard Davenport-Hines, copyright © 1995 by Pantheon Press. Used by permission of Random House, Inc.

From *The New Mencken Letters*, ed. Carl Bode, Dial Press © 1977. Used by permission of Doubleday, a division of Random House.

An excerpt from *The Diaries of Dawn Powell*, by Dawn Powell, published by Steerforth Press of South Royalton, Vermont. Copyright © 1995 by The Estate of Dawn Powell.

An excerpt from *The Literary Correspondence of Donald Davidson and Allen Tate*, edited by John Tyree Fain and Thomas Daniel Young, copyright © 1974 by permission of The University of Georgia Press.

Excerpts from *Hemingway at Auction: 1930–1973*, edited by Matthew J. Bruccoli and C. E. Frazer, Copyright © 1973 (Gale); University of South Carolina, 1999. Reprinted by permission of The University of South Carolina Press.

Excerpts from *The Only Thing that Counts: The Ernest Hemingway/Maxwell Perkins Correspondence, 1925–1947*, edited by Matthew J. Bruccoli (with the assistance of Robert W. Trogdon). Copyright © 1999. Reprinted by permission of The University of South Carolina Press.

Excerpts (pages 72, 150–151) from *The Starched Blue Sky of Spain* by Josephine Herbst. Copyright © 1991 by the Estate of Josephine Herbst. Reprinted by permission of HarperCollins Publishers Inc.

"Letter to Howard Cushman, June 21, 1967" and "Letter to William K. Zinsser, December 30, 1968" from *Letters of E. B. White, Collected and Edited by Dorothy Lobrano Guth.* Copyright © 1976 by E. B. White. Reprinted by permission of HarperCollins Publishers Inc.

Reprinted by permission of Farrar, Straus and Giroux, LLC:

Excerpts from *THE HABIT OF BEING,* edited by Sally Fitzgerald. Copyright © 1979 by Regina O'Connor.

Excerpts from *LETTERS ON LITERATURE AND POLITICS: 1917–1972* by Edmund Wilson, edited by Elena Wilson. Copyright © by Elena Wilson.

Excerpt from *Shakespeare and Company,* copyright © 1959 by Sylvia Beach and renewed 1987 by Frederic Beach Dennis, reprinted by permission of Harcourt, Inc.

Excerpt from *The Letters of Carl Sandburg,* Copyright © 1968 by Lillian Steichen Sandburg, Trustee, reprinted by permission of Harcourt, Inc.

Excerpt from *Selected Lettters of E. E. Cummings,* edited by Frederick Dupee and George Stade, copyright © 1969 by the Estate of Marion Morehouse Cummings, reprinted by permission of Harcourt, Inc.

Pages 98 and 108 from *Selected Letters of Dawn Powell: 1913–1965,* copyright © 1999 by Estate of Dawn Powell. Introduction and editing copyright © 1999 by Tim Page. Reprinted by permission of Henry Holt & Co., LLC.

Excerpts from letters of Alice B. Toklas, published in *Staying on Alone: Letters of Alice B. Toklas,* ed. Edward Burns, copyright ©1973, Liveright. Reprinted by permission of Edward Burns, executor of the estate of Alice B. Toklas.

Permission to quote Frank MacShane—John O'Hara courtesy of Nick MacShane.

PHOTOGRAPHIC CREDITS

"Paper ghosts . . . that's all they are." (From Marie Ponsot, "Restoring My House," *The Bird Catcher,* Alfred A. Knopf, 1998.)

All photographs of Ernest Hemingway [EH6945P, 728IN; 3998P; 3305P] appear through the courtesy of The Ernest Hemingway Photograph Collection of the John F. Kennedy Library.

Photograph of William Faulkner in 1960 by Jack Cofield from the Cofield Collection, Southern Media Archive, University of Mississippi, Archives and Special Collections.

W. C. Odiorne photo of William Faulkner: Harry Ransom Humanities Research Center, The University of Texas at Austin.

Photograph of Sherwood Anderson courtesy of Sherwood Anderson Papers, The Newberry Library, Chicago, with the permission also of Charles E. Modlin and Hilbert H. Campbell, Trustees.

Photograph of Gertrude Stein, Alice B. Toklas, and Carl Van Vechten by Carl Van Vechten, with permission of the Van Vechten Trust. Permission also granted by the Estate of Gertrude Stein, through its Literary Executor, Mr. Stanford Gann, Jr. of Levin & Gann, PA. And with the permission of the Yale Collection of American Literature, Beinecke Rare Book and Manuscript Library, Yale University.

Studio portrait of F. Scott Fitzgerald, courtesy of Rosemary Mizener Colt from Arthur Mizener, *Scott Fitzgerald and His World.*

Photographs of Edmund Wilson and John Peale Bishop from "The New Generation in Literature," *Vanity Fair*, February 1922.

Photograph of Kay Boyle and Harry Crosby from the Kay Boyle Papers, by permission of the Special Collection Research Center, Morris Library, Southern Illinois University, Carbondale, Illinois.

Photograph of Sinclair Lewis by Arnold Genthe (c. 1916). Reproduced from the Collections of the LIBRARY OF CONGRESS.

Photograph of T. S. Eliot by Barry Hyams (1954). Reproduced from the Collections of the LIBRARY OF CONGRESS.

Photograph of Eudora Welty. Reproduced from the Collections of the LIBRARY OF CONGRESS.

Photograph of Dawn Powell (1940). Reproduced from the Collections of the LIBRARY OF CONGRESS.

Photograph of Glenway Wescott, Malcolm Cowley, and Allen Tate on their election in the American Academy of Arts and Letters (1964). Reproduced from the Collections of the LIBRARY OF CONGRESS.

Photograph of Archibald MacLeish as Librarian of Congress (c. 1941). Reproduced from the Collections of the LIBRARY OF CONGRESS.

INDEX

Absalom, Absalom! (Faulkner), 110
  Fadiman on, 102
  Spain and, 98
Across the River and Into the Trees (Hemingway), 139
  Capote on, 166
  Dos Passos on, 47
  Faulkner on, 166
  Lewis, Sinclair, caricatured in, 114
  O'Hara on, 132
  White, E. B., on, 143
Aiken, Conrad, 58–59, 104
Aldington, Richard, 104, 105
Algonquin group, 15, 48, 118, 119
Algren, Nelson, 56, 135–36
Alimov, Sergei, 66
Anderson, Sherwood, 23–29, 85, 122
  Faulkner and, 24, 25, 26, 27–29, 42, 48, 110, 114, 131
  Hemingway and, 23–28, 29–30, 31, 34, 36, 63, 137
  The Torrents of Spring (Hemingway) as parody of, 26, 36, 43, 49, 54, 137
As I Lay Dying (Faulkner), 90, 110
  British publication of, 113
  Caldwell on, 85
  Dos Passos on, 48
  Hemingway on, 159
  Porter, Katherine Anne, on, 116
Asch, Nathan, 44
The Atlantic Monthly, 67
Auden, W. H., 142, 146

Baird, Helen, 79
Baker, Carlos, 128
Baker, Josephine, 97
Balzac, Honoré de, 88
Barnes, Djuna, 25
Barnett, Uncle Ned, 75, 77
Basso, Hamilton, 28, 74, 131–32
"The Battler" (Hemingway), 76
Beach, Sylvia, 71
  Hemingway and, 56–58
  Shakespeare and Company of, 56, 57, 58, 113, 115–16, 125
"The Bear" (Faulkner), 124
  Dos Passos on, 48
  Hemingway on, 165

Bellow, Saul, 139, 149
Benchley, Robert, 119
Benedict, Ruth, 97–98
Benet, Stephen, 115
Bennett, Arnold, 113
Berenson, Bernard, 100
Biala, Janice, 81
Bird, William, 92–93
Bishop, Elizabeth, 107–8
Bishop, John Peale, 39, 49, 51, 77–79
Black, Marvin, 161
Black Sun Press, 59
Blast (magazine), 112
Bloom, Harold, 142
Bloomsbury Group, 112
Blotner, Joseph, 48–49
Bogan, Louise, 97–98
Boni, Albert & Charles, 24, 25, 49
Boulder, Colorado, writers' conference in, 104
Bowen, Stella, 154, 155
Boyle, Kay, 22, 122–23
Breit, Harvey, 29, 95, 99–100, 163–64
Bromfield, Louis, 22
Brooks, Cleanth, 86–87
Brown, William Slater, 99
Bryher, Winifred, 52, 105
Burke, Kenneth, 141–43

Cabell, James Branch, 74
Caldwell, Erskine, 29, 84–86
  Faulkner and, 35, 81
  on Nobel Prize, 85–86
Callaghan, Morley, 70
Capa, Robert, 128
Cape & Smith, 80
Capote, Truman, 56–57, 166
Carpenter, Meta, 35–36, 79
Cather, Willa, 57, 136
Cerf, Bennett, 110
Cézanne, Paul, 23
Champion, Myra, 47
Charles Scribner and Sons. *See also* Perkins, Max; Scribner, Charles; *Scribner's* (magazine)
  Hemingway and, 36–37, 54, 64, 67
  Wilson and, 66–67

Charlottesville, Virginia, writers' conference
    in, 80–81
Cheney, Brainard "Lon," 81, 151
Church, Henry, 102–3
Civil War (American), 75, 120
Clark, Walter Van Tilburg, 110
Cocteau, Jean, 60
Colum, Mary, 40
Compson, Quentin, 62
Confederacy, 86–87
    "The Lost Cause" of, 74
Congress for Cultural Freedom, 146
Conrad, Joseph, 39, 94
Contact (magazine), 52
Copenhaver, Laura, 27
Costello, Tim, 128, 141
Covici, Pascal, 130
Cowley, Malcolm, 22, 66, 141–43
    The Portable Faulkner edited by, 13, 124,
        141, 145, 160, 161
Crane, Hart, 22, 25, 59, 61, 88, 98–99
Crane, Joan St. C., 147
Crane, Stephen, 47–48
Cromwell, Dorothea, 61
Cromwell, Gladys, 61
Crosby, Harry, 59–62
Cummings, E. E., 22, 25, 71, 101, 105–6
Cummings, Saxe, 129–30
Cushman, Howard, 143

Dadaists, 65
Dance, Beatrice, 41
Dardis, Tom, 35, 36
Davidson, Donald, 73, 82–84, 145
"Death Drag" (Faulkner), 44
Death in the Afternoon (Hemingway), 109
    Dos Passos on, 45–46, 51
    Eastman on, 27
    Faulkner referenced in, 159–60
    film version of, 97
    The New Yorker parody of, 143
    Perkins on, 51
    Saroyan on, 134–35
Desnos, Robert, 154, 155
The Dial (magazine), 96
Dinesen, Isak, 100
"The Doctor and the Doctor's Wife" (Hem-
    ingway), 76
Donoghue, Denis, 142
Doolittle, Hilda (H.D.), 52, 96, 104–5
Dos Passos, John, 13, 29, 41, 42–49, 65, 109,
    115, 126
    Faulkner and, 47, 48–49, 69–70, 110, 162
    Hemingway and, 42–44, 45–48, 51, 68, 70–
        71, 101, 120, 121, 126–27
    National Institute of Arts and Letters gold
        medal won by, 48
    on Wolfe, 47
Dostoevsky, Fyodor, 68, 149
Double Dealer (magazine), 63, 104, 157, 159
Dreiser, Theodore, 110, 111, 114, 131, 144
"Dry September" (Faulkner), 77

DuBois, W. E. B., 75
Durand, Lionel, 105

Eastman, Max, 27, 41
Eby, Carl, 57
Egoist (magazine), 105
Eliot, T(homas) S(tearns), 25, 56, 91, 94–95,
    98, 118, 122
    anti-Semitism of, 44
    Faulkner influenced by, 95
    Fitzgerald and, 94–95
    Hemingway and, 94–95
Ellerman, Winifred. See Bryher, Winifred
Ellison, Ralph, 76–77, 139, 149–51
Esquire (magazine), 105–6
Expressionism, 65

The Fable (Faulkner), 124, 140, 165
Fadiman, Clifton, 87, 102
A Farewell to Arms (Hemingway), 106, 139
    Davidson on, 82–83, 84
    Dos Passos on, 45
    Fitzgerald on, 38
    MacLeish on, 50
    Powell on, 128
    Tate on, 81
    Wilson on, 64–65
    Wolfe on, 88
Farrell, James T., 144
Faulkner, Alabama, 62
Faulkner, Dean, 62
Feo, Rodriguez, 101
Fiedler, Leslie, 22
The Fifth Column (Hemingway), 66
Finca Vigia, as Hemingway's home, 78–79
Fitzgerald, F. Scott, 13, 22, 34–42, 62, 65, 70,
    77, 109, 131
    Eliot and, 94–95
    Faulkner and, 34–36, 38, 41–42
    Hemingway and, 34, 36–42, 44, 51, 69, 80,
        81, 94–95, 111, 112
    Perkins and, 34, 36–37, 38–40, 41
    Wilson and, 67–68
Fitzgerald, Robert, 151
Fitzgerald, Sally, 151
Flags in the Dust (Faulkner), 45
Flaubert, Gustav, 81, 88
Foote, Shelby, 28
For Whom the Bell Tolls (Hemingway), 110
    Faulkner on, 166
    film rights for, 106
    Fitzgerald on, 41
    individual v. world in, 123
    Lewis, Sinclair, on, 115
    Schwartz on, 149
Ford, Ford Madox, 31, 93, 155
Forty Nine Stories (Hemingway), 109–10
Fowler, Gene, 35
Frank, Waldo, 25, 79
Franklin, Sydney, 152–53
Freud, Sigmund, 25
Frost, Robert, 103–4, 109

The Fugitive (periodical), 82, 145. *See also* Vanderbilt University

The Garden of Eden (Hemingway), 56, 140
Gauss, Christian, 64
Gellhorn, Martha, 78
Giacometti, Alberto, 154
Gide, André, 68
Gingrich, Arnold, 105
Glasgow, Ellen, 74, 80–81
Go Down, Moses (Faulkner)
    Ellison on, 76–77
    racial dilemma in, 124
    Wilson on, 69–70
Gold, Michael, 115
Gordon, Caroline, 74, 80–82, 116
Great Depression, 109, 123
The Great Gatsby (Fitzgerald), 34
Green Hills of Africa (Hemingway), 26–27, 66, 110
Green, Paul, 28, 73
Greene, Graham, 151
Gregory, Alyse, 63
Guthrie, Ramon, 154–55

Haas, Robert, 45, 106
The Hamlet (Faulkner), 124, 140
Hammett, Dashiell, 35, 124–25
Hardy, Thomas, 81, 94
Harper's (magazine), 77
Hartley, Marsden, 30
Harvard University, 59
Hawks, Howard, 35
H.D. *See* Doolittle, Hilda (H.D.)
Hellmann, Lillian, 124–25
Hemingway, Ursula, 101
Herbst, Josephine, 120–21, 126
Herrmann, John, 96, 120
Hersey, John, 128
Heyward, DuBose, 74, 111
Hicks, Granville, 102
"Hills Like White Elephants" (Hemingway), 53
Hivnor, Robert, 149
Hollywood
    Faulkner and, 15, 35–36, 106, 124
    Hemingway and, 15, 97, 106, 119
Hotel des Artistes (New York), 59
Hughes, Richard, 113
Hurston, Zora Lee, 147
Huxley, Aldous, 152

Imagist school, 105
"In Another Country" (Hemingway), 64
In Our Time (Hemingway), 54
    Anderson on, 24
    Bogan on, 97–98
    Dos Passos on, 43
    Hellmann on, 125
    MacLeish on, 51–52
    Morris on, 137–38
    Schneider on, 54
    Wilson on, 63–64

"Indian Camp" (Hemingway), 76
Intruder in the Dust (Faulkner), 33, 124
    Dos Passos on, 47, 48
    Ellison on, 77
    Wilson on, 69–70
Islands in the Stream (Hemingway), 140
Ivancich, Adriana, 78

James, Henry, 59, 105, 122
Jeffers, Robinson, 25, 97
Jenkins, Susan, 99
Johnson, Else, 79
Jones, James, 37, 139
Joyce, James, 25, 56, 59, 65, 92, 122
    Faulkner and, 149
    Hemingway and, 57–58, 60, 111
    on McAlmon, 58

Karl, Frederick, 57, 167–68
Karmel, Ilona, 51
Kashkeen, Ivan, 55
Katz, Florine, 66–67
Katzke, Georg, 112
Kazin, Alfred, 70, 71
Kazin, Pearl, 108
Keats, John, 39–40, 104
Kemler, Edgar, 112
Kenyon College, *The Kenyon Review* published by, 87
Key West, Florida, 100–101, 120
"The Killers" (Hemingway), 50, 55, 64, 99, 129
Kipling, Rudyard, 33
Kreymborg, Alfred, 30

Lanham, Buck, 162, 163
Lardner, Ring, 38, 119
The Last Tycoon (Fitzgerald), 34–35
Lawrence, D. H., 59, 105, 108
Lawrence, Seymour, 117
League of American Writers, 98
Lewis, Sinclair, 110, 154, 155
    Nobel Prize won by, 109, 114–15
Lewis, Wyndham, 50, 112–14
Light in August (Faulkner), 110
    Nabokov on, 68–69
    O'Connor on, 152
    race in, 77
    Wilder on, 125–26
Lindsay, Vachel, 61
Liveright, Horace, 24, 25–26, 45, 49, 54, 125
Loeb, Harold, 44
Longstreet, Stephen, 35
Loos, Anita, 57
"The Lost Generation," 22, 24, 32, 92
Lowell, Amy, 52
Lowell, Robert, 108, 146
Luce, Henry, 22

MacLeish, Archibald, 56, 59, 77
    on Faulkner, 51

on Hemingway, 49–52
Pulitzer Prize won by, 49
Mailer, Norman, 139
Mann, Thomas, 68
The Mansion (Faulkner), 140, 146
The Marble Faun (Faulkner), 23
Mariani, Paul, 95, 96
Mark Twain. *See* Twain, Mark
Marquis, Don, 144
Marshall, S. A., 100
Mason, Jane, 78
Matisse, Henri, 23
Maugham, Somerset, 118
Maxwell, William, 132
McAlmon, Robert, 22, 96, 105, 122–23
Hemingway and, 52–54, 93, 96
Joyce on, 58
McCarthy, Mary, 148–49
McCown, Father J. H., 151
McCoy, Horace, 35
Mellow, James, 32
Men without Women (Hemingway), 99, 111, 166
Mencken, H. L., 35, 44, 111–12, 136
Meredith, George, 13
Miller, Henry, 22, 111, 118
Mitchell, Margaret, 109
Mizener, Arthur, 69
Modernists, 18
Monnier, Adrienne, 56, 58
Monroe, Harriet, 105
Moore, John Warner, 97
Moore, Marianne, 96–97, 104, 107–8
Moore, Merrill, 73
Morris, Wright, 136–38
Mosquitoes (Faulkner), 23, 26
A Moveable Feast (Hemingway), 139, 167
Stein, Gertrude, in, 31, 32
"Mr. and Mrs. Elliott" (Hemingway), 50
Mudrick, Marvin, 86
Murphy, Gerald, 38, 126
Murphy, Sara, 38, 101, 126, 128
Murray, Albert, 150
Mussolini, Benito, 93
"My Old Man" (Hemingway), 53

Nabokov, Vladimir, 68–69
Nashville, Tennessee, 73
National Book Award
Bishop, Elizabeth, awarded, 107
Faulkner awarded, 101–2
Stevens awarded, 101–2
National Institute of Arts and Letters, Dos Passos awarded, 48
Naturalism, 65
New Criticism, 142
New Masses (magazine), 27
New Orleans, Louisiana, 25, 28, 57, 63, 73, 79, 157
The New Republic, 65, 145
New York Herald-Tribune, 161
New York Review of Books, 69, 86

New York Times, 76, 102, 103, 132
The New Yorker, 25, 102, 122, 131–32, 143
Nin, Anaïs, 118
Nobel Prize
Caldwell on, 85–86
Faulkner and, 86, 104, 115, 139, 163
Hemingway and, 86, 99–100, 114–15, 139, 163, 165
Lewis, Sinclair, awarded, 109, 114–15
Steinbeck awarded, 13, 85–86, 131

Oak Park, Illinois, 74, 100, 119
O'Connor, Flannery, 151–52
O'Hara, John, 127, 128, 132–33
Faulkner and, 35, 132
Hemingway and, 132–33, 141
The Old Man and the Sea (Hemingway), 139
Bishop, Elizabeth, on, 108
Faulkner on, 151, 164–65
Steinbeck on, 129
Oldham, Estelle, 79
O'Neill, Eugene, 25, 30, 65, 114, 131–32
Oxford, Mississippi, 24, 28, 74, 75, 89, 124

Paris, France, 21–71, 77, 80, 81, 84, 112, 118, 146
Parker, Dorothy, 44, 118–19
Algonquin group of, 15, 48, 118, 119
Faulkner and, 119
Hemingway and, 119, 126
Pecile, Jordon, 117
Perelman, S. J., 144
Perkins, Max. *See also* Charles Scribner and Sons
Eastman and, 27, 41
Fitzgerald and, 34, 36–37, 38–40, 41
Hemingway and, 27, 36–37, 38–40, 41, 51, 54, 64–65, 66, 67, 127
Wolfe and, 38, 39–40, 87
Pfeiffer, Pauline, 78, 106, 119, 126, 155
Pfeiffer, Virginia, 126
Picasso, Pablo, 23
Pivano, Fernanda, 33
Poe, Edgar Allan, 165
Poetry (magazine), 92, 105
Poore, Charles, 165
Pope, James, 130
The Portable Faulkner, Cowley as editor of, 13, 124, 141, 145, 160, 161
Porter, Katherine Anne, 60, 96, 99, 109, 146
on Faulkner, 116
Hemingway and, 78, 115–17
Porter, Paul, 116
Postmodernists, 18
Pound, Ezra, 24, 25, 52, 56, 92–93, 105, 112, 118
anti-Semitism of, 44
confinement of, 92
Faulkner and, 30, 92, 97
Hemingway and, 36, 53–54, 56, 92, 93, 94, 95, 96
Imagist school of, 105
on Liveright, 25–26

Powell, Dawn, 126–30
Prall, Elizabeth, 24, 89
Proust, Marcel, 28, 154
Pulitzer Prize
    Frost awarded, 109
    MacLeish awarded, 49
"A Pursuit Race" (Hemingway), 50
Pushkin, Alexander, 68, 69
Pylon (Faulkner), 44, 49, 105
    Hemingway on, 159, 165

Random House, 45, 106, 110, 150
Ransom, John Crowe, 22, 73, 82, 87, 141
Rawlings, Marjorie Kinnan, 37
Red Leaves (Faulkner), 138
Requiem for a Nun (Faulkner), 125
Reynolds, Michael, 32, 34, 74
Rice, Grantland, 128
Richardson, Hadley, 23, 42–43, 74, 78, 119,
    155
Richmond, Virginia, 73
Roberts, Elizabeth Madox, 74
Robinson, Edwin Arlington, 104
Robles, Jose, 4
Roche, John, 151
Rodin, François Auguste, 23
Roethke, Theodore, 97, 107
Romanticism, 118
Root, Waverly, 122
Ross, Harold, 22
Ross, Lillian, 152–54
Royal Air Force (Canada), Faulkner in, 23

Sale, Richard, 85
Salinger, J. D., 139
Salmagundi (magazine), 159
San Francisco, California, 21
Sanctuary (Faulkner), 35, 90, 111
    Bishop, John Peale, on, 78
    as controversial, 110
    Eliot's influence on, 95
    Hammett on, 124
    Hemingway on, 65, 159
    Mencken on, 112
    Miller on, 118
    Stein, Gertrude, and, 33
    Tate on, 86–87
    Walker on, 134
    Wilson on, 65
Sandburg, Carl, 99–100
Saroyan, William, 134–35
Sartoris (Faulkner), 26
Sartre, Jean-Paul, 160
Saturday Review, 55, 161
Saxon, Lyle, 48
Sayre, Joel, 35
Schneider, Isidor, 54–55, 159
Schwartz, Delmore, 149
Scopes Trial (Dayton), 73
Scott, Evelyn, 79–80, 88
Scribner's (magazine), 64, 88–89

Scribner, Charles, 36. *See also* Charles
    Scribner and Sons
Shakespeare and Company, 56, 57, 58, 113,
    115–16, 125
Shakespeare, William, 104, 132
Sheean, Vincent, 128
Shelley, Percy Bysshe, 104
Sherwin, Vernon, 111
Sherwood Anderson & Other Creoles (Faulk-
    ner/Spratling), 26
"The Short Happy Life of Francis Ma-
    comber" (Hemingway), 66, 110
Smith, Bill, 23, 42, 99
Smith, Katy, 42–43
Smith, Kenley, 23–24
Smith, Y.K., 42
"The Snows of Kilimanjaro" (Hemingway),
    109–10
    Fitzgerald reference in, 40–41
Soldier's Pay (Faulkner)
    Anderson on, 24, 25
    as first novel, 23, 24
    Hemingway on, 159
    Schneider on, 159
The Sound and the Fury (Faulkner), 90
    anti-Semitism in, 44–45
    British publication of, 113
    Porter, Katherine Anne, on, 116
    racial dilemma in, 77, 124
    Scott on, 79–80
Southern writers, 73–90, 145
Spanish Civil War, 46, 98, 110, 120–21, 166
The Spanish Earth (documentary film), 46
Spender, Stephen, 58
Spenser, Edmund, 104
Spratling, William, 57
Stein, Gertrude, 24, 29–32, 52, 137, 149
    Faulkner and, 30, 33, 81
    Hemingway and, 29–32, 33–34, 44, 48, 50,
        56, 63, 67, 69, 80, 95, 112, 113, 122
    "The Lost Generation" and, 22, 24, 32, 92
    on Paris, France, 22
    Toklas and, 30, 31–34, 56, 81
Stein, Jean, 79, 130
Steinbeck, John, 13, 28, 109, 128–31, 132, 157
    Faulkner and, 129–30, 131, 132, 162
    Hemingway and, 86, 128–29, 130–31, 132
    Nobel Prize won by, 13, 85–86, 131
Stevens, Wallace
    Faulkner and, 101–2, 103, 168
    Hemingway and, 100–101, 103, 168
    National Book Award won by, 101–2
Stevenson, Anne, 108
Steward, Samuel, 33–34
Stewart, Donald Ogden, 44, 119
Stone, Phil, 89–90, 159
Story (magazine), 147
Styron, William, 139
The Sun Also Rises (Hemingway), 54, 125
    Aiken on, 59
    anti-Semitism and, 44
    caricatures in, 43–44, 56

Crane, Hart, on, 99
Dos Passos on, 43
Faulkner on, 166
as first novel, 23
Fitzgerald on, 37–38
Lewis, Sinclair, on, 115
MacLeish on, 49–50
Miller on, 118
Perkins and, 36, 37
Schneider on, 54–55
Stein, Gertrude, and, 32
Steinbeck on, 129
Teasdale on, 20
Wilson on, 64
Symbolism, 65

Tate, Allen, 65, 73, 77, 82, 87, 141, 145, 146
on Faulkner, 78, 80, 86–87
on Hemingway, 78, 81, 83–84
Teasdale, Sara
suicide of, 61
on The Sun Also Rises (Hemingway), 20
"Ten Indians" (Hemingway), 76
Tender Is the Night (Fitzgerald), 94–95
This Side of Paradise (Fitzgerald), 77
Thompson, Lawrance, 104
Three Stories and Ten Poems (Hemingway),
     23, 63, 92
"The Three-Day Blow" (Hemingway), 60
Thurber, James, 140–41, 153–54
Tillett, Dorothy, 111
To Have and Have Not (Hemingway), 66, 110
Toklas, Alice B., 33–34
on Faulkner, 33, 81
Hemingway and, 31–34, 44, 56, 153
Stein, Gertrude, and, 30, 31–34, 56, 81
Toronto Star, 22, 114
The Torrents of Spring (Hemingway)
Dos Passos on, 43
Liveright's rejection of, 43, 49
as parody of Anderson, 26, 36, 43, 49, 54,
     137
Schneider on, 54
The Town (Faulkner), 140
Transatlantic Review, Hemingway writing
     for, 36
True at First Light (Hemingway), 76, 78, 140,
     167
Truman, Harry, 22
Twain, Mark, 24, 29, 31, 137, 138, 150

Universal Pictures, 97
University of Virginia, 42, 165
"Up in Michigan" (Hemingway), 30–31
Updike, John, 15

Van Vechten, Carl, 33
Vanderbilt University, 73, 82. See also The Fu-
     gitive (periodical)
Vendler, Helen, 13
Vogel, James, 93

Walker, Margaret, 134
Wallace, DeWitt, 22
Warren, Robert Penn, 73–74
Faulkner and, 86, 104, 145–46
on Hemingway, 145–46
Wasson, Ben, 79
Welles, Orson, 133
Welsh, Mary, 78, 124
Welty, Eudora, 147–48
Wescott, Glenway, 56, 121, 146
West, Nathaniel, 35, 109
Westcott, Glenway, 37
Wharton, Edith, 20, 44, 122
Wheeler, Monroe, 101, 116
White, E. B., 143–44
White, Katherine, 140–41
Whitman, Walt, 24, 98–99, 118
The Wild Palms (Faulkner), 62
Wilder, Thornton, 29, 41, 56, 115, 125–26
on Faulkner, 125–26
Hemingway and, 111
Williams, Joan, 79
Williams, Tennessee, 148
Williams, William Carlos, 52, 79, 95–96, 104
Hemingway and, 53, 92, 95–96
Wilson, Edmund, 22, 47, 62–71, 77, 97, 118,
     126, 131
Faulkner and, 63, 65, 68–70
Fitzgerald and, 67–68
Hemingway and, 62–68, 69, 70–71
Nabokov and, 68–69
Scribner's and, 66–67
Winner Take Nothing (Hemingway), 65. See
     also specific stories
Winters, Yvor, 99
Wister, Owen, 159
Wolfe, Thomas, 13, 28, 29, 37, 41–42, 65, 87–
     90, 109, 115, 131
anti-Semitism of, 44
Dos Passos on, 47
Faulkner and, 89–90, 162, 165–66
Hemingway and, 28, 39–40, 47, 88–89, 90,
     136, 162
Perkins and, 38, 39–40, 87
Woolf, Virginia, 152
in Bloomsbury Group, 112
Woollcott, Alexander, 118
Wordsworth, William, 39
World War I, 21, 22, 45, 59, 87, 154
World War II, 122, 123–24, 154
Wright, Richard, 109, 133–34
Wylie, Elinor, 57, 60

Yale Literary Magazine, 115
Yale University, 49
Yoknapatawpha County, 113, 164
Young, Stark, 74, 145
Faulkner and, 57, 80–81, 89–90

Zinsser, William, 144